W9-AXQ-415

quitting
the
nairobi
trio

ALSO BY JIM KNIPFEL

Slackjaw

JEREMY P. TARCHER · PUTNAM

a member of

Penguin Putnam Inc.

New York

quitting

the

nairobi

trio

jim knipfel

In deference to my friends, subjects, and fellow patients, I have taken care to alter names and most identifying features.

Jeremy P. Tarcher/Putnam
a member of
Penguin Putnam Inc.
375 Hudson Street
New York, NY 10014
www.penguinputnam.com

Portions of this book, in different form, have appeared in the following
publications: *Browbeat, New York Press,* and *Welcomat.*

The author gratefully acknowledges permission from Taradam Music Inc. to
reprint lyrics from "Pure Imagination" by Anthony Newley (ca. 1970–1971).

Library of Congress Cataloging-in-Publication Data

Knipfel, Jim.
    Quitting the Nairobi Trio / Jim Knipfel.
       p.   cm.
    Includes bibliographical references.
    ISBN 1-58542-027-1
    1. Knipfel, Jim—Mental health.   2. Psychiatric hospital patients—
Minnesota—Biography.   3. Mentally ill—Minnesota—Biography.
4. Psychiatric hospital care.   I. Title
RC464.K65 A3   2000   00-021773
616.89'0092—dc21
    [B]

Printed in the United States of America
10   9   8   7   6   5   4   3   2   1

This book is printed on acid-free paper. ♾

Book design by Claire Naylon Vaccaro

FOR DEREK S. B. DAVIS,
compadre and goofball,
who always liked that story

contents

quitting
the
nairobi
trio

There's a song Gene Wilder sings in *Willy Wonka and the Chocolate Factory* that says, in part, "If you want to view paradise, simply look around and view it." As the esteemed candy magnate, Wilder goes on to sing: "There is no life I know to compare with pure imagination. Living there, you'll be free, if you truly wish to be."

I never took Mr. Wonka's advice. I preferred the ugly world.

Fact of the matter is, it wasn't until I was in my twenties, and saw the movie for the eighth or ninth time, that it struck me that Willy Wonka was condoning, even encouraging, schizophrenia as a viable life-style option. And while very few of the schizophrenics I've come to know over the years have chosen to populate their new worlds with candy-laden trees and chocolate rivers, a few have, indeed, been tormented by stern, finger-waggling orange midgets.

Most people get creepy and nervous when I offhandedly mention that I've spent a goodly amount of time in the bughouse. I can understand that. It's not their fault.

It's a topic most normals don't care to face—especially since nearly everything they know about mental institutions comes from movies, television, and the occasional book about the subject. *One Flew over the Cuckoo's Nest, Titicut Follies, I Never Promised You a Rose Garden*, and *The Cramps Live at the Napa State Mental Hospital* are all remarkable bits of work. And for the most part, they were also reasonably accurate portrayals—for their times—of the cruel warehousing and abuse to which the mentally ill have been subjected.

One thing these documents rarely admit, however, is that there are a few folks who (maybe just because they're insane) honestly enjoy being where they are, and would never want to leave. I have run into more than a few such individuals, in fact, through my own travels in and out of these places. And I, for one, enjoyed my time on a locked ward in Minneapolis.

I wasn't exploding with joy each minute of every day I spent there. That would be nuts, and I'd probably still be there today if that had been the case. There were elements of horror and menace—though of quite a different nature from what you run into on a daily basis living in New York, as I do. There was also devastating boredom to contend with—which, for me, was much worse than the horror and the menace. But the food was okay and my bed was comfortable.

In the late 1980s, when these particular events took

place, mental institutions had changed a great deal since the days of the hellholes we're used to hearing about. They were cleaner, for one thing, and more was known about the nature and causes of mental illness. Advancements in psychotropic drugs and other treatments had, to a great extent, done away with straitjackets and shock treatment. Not completely, but almost.

According to the Center for Mental Health Services, an estimated 41 million Americans will suffer some sort of mental disorder in their lifetime. Of those, 5.5 million will suffer a form of extreme psychological trauma, such as schizophrenia, autism, or immobilizing depression—something severe enough to require medical treatment.

Statistics for the number of people actually put away for a while are hard to come by, given the vast range of hospitals, institutions, independent treatment centers, and halfway houses scattered around the country. Then there are the people with serious mental problems who go untreated—the estimated 600,000 nuts among the nation's homeless population, and the quarter-million figured to be housed in our prisons, to name a few. I have no social comment to make here. My only point is that there are a hell of a lot of us out there.

I'm often asked if my stays in various psych wards changed me at all. I'm of two minds (so to speak) when it comes to answering that question. Yes, it changed me. The analogies between prisons and psych wards are undeniable.

It's impossible to go through an extended incarceration, isolated from the rest of the "real world," separated from the people you care about and can talk to in a normal fashion without being affected. A person cannot be surrounded by men and women who are considered unfit for general society, and not be changed in some fundamental way.

At the same time, though, on an individual level, if the implied question is "Did it help you?" or "Did it cure you?" then the answer is *Pah!*

I was locked away in that ward in Minneapolis because I was a self-destructive young man. Months later, I left the ward a self-destructive young man. All these years later, I'm older, grumpier, too tired—and to be honest, too curious about the things going on around me—to be bothered with the effort of trying to take my own life anymore.

I do, however, continue to find myself in situations that might raise the eyebrows of the well-adjusted.

Parts of this book recount a series of events, as I perceived them, that followed an intentional drug overdose. In those sections (they're pretty obvious), I was not writing science fiction, nor was I trying to be "surreal," "postmodern," or even "silly-assed." I was not trying to pull a Burroughs or a Castaneda or a Cendrars, and I didn't drop acid before I started typing.

From my perspective, these events are as real to me as

lunch. They may have been simple hallucinations. They may represent what my doctors later called a "psychotic break" ("If you want to view paradise, simply look around and view it . . ."). Or as I believed for some time afterward, I may have died after that overdose and gone to Hell for a few days. My doctor in the ICU did hint that he had lost me temporarily.

To put it in a slightly different way: I've had dreams and I've had hallucinations, but they've always faded in time. The events of those three particular days are lodged in my mind with a tenacity and clarity unattributable to any simple unconscious reaction in the brain's biochemistry. I can remember the details of those days, which exist somewhere in the usually murky zone of memory, better than I can remember what I did yesterday.

And because of the nature of what I experienced, well, let's just say it's the kind of thing that sticks with you.

For the record, I have included excerpts from the preliminary and official reports of my check-in examinations, one by an intern and one by the emergency room physician. The examinations were conducted while I was in the midst of my frolics. The reports reveal certain contradictions in my own account, as well as a few things I was not aware of before obtaining these reports, almost fifteen years after the stated events.

One of the things they reveal that I never knew was

that I had been diagnosed as having "mixed-personality disorder." No medical professional had ever told me that to my face. In technical terms, a personality disorder is, by definition, "an enduring pattern of inner experience and behavior which persists over several years and deviates markedly from the expectations of one's home culture." There are several distinct categories—antisocial personality, dependent personality, paranoid, schizoid, schizotypal. Labeling me as suffering a "mixed-personality disorder" meant that I didn't fit neatly into any one of these categories—or fit in neatly much of anywhere else, either. I was comforted to hear that.

Old habits are hard to break if you want to go to the bother of breaking them. In my case, the habits and impulses that landed me in the hospital in the first place have mostly subsided over the ensuing years. I've had better things to do. To some, this might be called "growing up." I prefer to call it "moving on."

Be all that as it may, I still stand by my account. I did trail Satan around for a bit, and I did perform *Tristan und Isolde* all by myself.

Point being, I guess, to pass along a warning that things get pretty fucking weird.

But don't they always?

JMK
Brooklyn, 2000

This fragmented body ... usually manifests itself in dreams when the movement of the analysis encounters a certain level of aggressive disintegration in the individual. It then appears in the form of disjointed limbs, or of those organs represented in exoscopy, growing wings and taking up arms for intestinal persecutions—the very same that the visionary Hieronymus Bosch has fixed, for all time, in painting.

—JACQUES LACAN,
"The Mirror Stage as Formative of the I
as Revealed in Psychoanalytic Experience"

People always call a madhouse "someplace," don't they?
—NORMAN BATES, *Psycho*

Nothing in moderation.
—ERNIE KOVACS

1 · *Where I Am?*

It's never easy telling your mother that you've failed again. Especially when she seems to have a pretty clear notion of how, and she's sitting across the room from where you lie strapped to a hospital bed. I had let her down—I'd let both my folks down—again. It was a bad habit of mine. I didn't try to, Lord knows. It just sort of happened, no matter how much I cared for them.

I was in the intensive care unit of Minneapolis General Medical Center. I was bound to a bed in a small room whose walls were formed by stiff gray curtains. Through a wide opening in the curtains, I could see a doorway and half a desk across a wide corridor. Men in white uniforms were pushing carts and beds back and forth. There were clatterings, beepings, mixed voices, the rolling of metal wheels on a tile floor.

The guttural German screams that had woken me had finally been silenced. It had taken me a few minutes to comprehend that it was my own voice I'd been hearing, yelling in a language I hadn't spoken in two years.

"*In jener Gegend reist man jetzt nicht gut!*" erupted from my mouth as my surroundings bled into cohesion earlier that day. "*Und hast du Geist, sei doppelt auf der Hut!*"

I was screaming Nietzsche, I soon realized. Worse still, I was screaming Nietzsche in *rhyme*.

"*War ich krank? Bin ich gewesen? Und wer ist mein Arzt gewesen? Wie vergass ich alle das!*"

Needles were in both my arms. Something long and narrow and sharp had been inserted into the end of my penis. My wrists and ankles were held in place by leather bands.

I'm in a hospital screaming in German, strapped down and screaming in German—by God, I must've gone completely insane.

That epiphany filled me with relief. I'd be able to spend the rest of my days in an institution, saying funny things. I'd be fed and have a place to sleep. I'd have freedom to do with my time whatever I pleased, say whatever I pleased, so long as it made no sense. I had it made. I was rid of useless daily obligations. I'd join the ranks of the visionaries who'd died in madhouses—like Artaud and the Marquis de Sade.

Unfortunately, everything caught up with me then.

Damn.

I opened my eyes more fully to find my parents sitting in chairs at the foot of the bed. My father's eyes were emptied wide and his normally smiling face was drawn and tired. He looked even worse than my mother, who appeared to be waiting uncomfortably for me to yell again.

"Hi, you two," I said in English, without rhyming.

My father snapped to attention. He was a burly man, six feet tall and two hundred pounds, with short graying hair thinning in the back. After a moment the broad smile I was more used to broke across his face. He jumped out of his chair and stepped to the bedside.

"How are you feeling?" he asked, tentatively—still uncertain, it seemed, whether I recognized him or not.

"I think I need a shave." I wiggled my sore arms the best I could.

"Do you know who I am?"

My mother sat up straighter. Under the silvery red curls swept back from her forehead, her eyebrows were poised and curious. She pulled her blue winter jacket tighter around her shoulders, watching us.

"George James Knipfel," I replied, making sure I got everything right. Even my tongue felt tied down. My father let go a loud whoop and slapped his heavy hands. He swung toward my mother, who was crying again, then back to me.

"Last time I asked you that"—he was fighting his own tears—"you told me I was the Man in Blue. You said, 'Whatcha gonna do 'bout the Man in Blue?' "

It was all very embarrassing. I had been rhyming for a while.

I had four intravenous drips hooked into my body. My

parents explained that I had spent the past three days in a delirium, lashing at nurses, swinging at doctors, trying to pull needles out of my arms. Late the night before, I'd started in with the German.

Whatever I had done to my body, they told me, had caused my kidneys to shut down. The only reason I was alive was the fact that I had stumbled into the hallway of my apartment building and made a lot of noise. One of my neighbors, thinking I was on PCP, had called the building manager, who in turn called the cops.

"We went to your apartment yesterday," my mother said softly, after my parents had both pulled their chairs closer to the head of the bed. Her voice was broken and exhausted. "What were those pills?"

The pills. Oh, man.

"There is only one prospect worse than being chained to an intolerable existence," Arthur Koestler once wrote. "The nightmare of a botched attempt to end it."

"They were blue and green pills, all mixed together in a cup."

Five nights earlier, I had had a plan—one that made perfect sense. Having been through the suicide game so often since my early teens, and having seen the effect it had on the people I cared about and trusted, I concocted an alternative scheme that would provide the proper result, but without the excess guilt.

In the few moments when an honest voice spoke in my head, it was clear that it was cowardice that had kept me from going all the way before. I had never succeeded because I didn't have the nerve. That quiet voice, though, was usually shouted down by the hubris of youth, which after each failure screamed loudly and more proudly that I had survived again simply because I was too strong, that I could not be killed, that I was invincible.

Regardless of the voices, I kept at my repeated attempts into my twenties, when I was a philosophy graduate student at the University of Minnesota. There, apart from taking seminars, writing papers, and attending academic cocktail parties, my responsibilities involved teaching a handful of undergraduate classes.

Over the past weeks, a woman in her late forties who was taking one of my night courses, "Introduction to Humanities," had been leaving me obsessive love notes. I had found them in my office desk, in my notebooks—places she shouldn't have had access to. I suspected she was following me around as well. I had no evidence of this beyond the notes, but those were enough for me to believe that she was capable of many things.

My plan was simple—make it look like murder, and make it look like she did it.

I left her most recent scribbled note—"WHY won't you pay attention to ME!?"—on my desk at home. I placed a can of frozen orange juice in the kitchen sink to thaw. This would show any investigating officers that my life had been continuing along its steady, uneventful path, that I had not expected anything weird to happen. Next I grabbed a steak knife, went to the front room of my apartment, removed my shirt, and slashed the knife through it three or four times.

I put the shirt back on, then reached behind myself with the knife. I felt for the slashes and tried to make corresponding cuts in the flesh of my back. My stalker had attacked me with the knife—I was trying to get away when she slashed at me from behind. When I fell on the knife, it would look as if she'd murdered me.

Mishima I was not, however. The "wounds" on my back turned out to be little more than scratch marks, because my arm couldn't reach very well. I couldn't even throw myself on the knife. I lacked the courage to drive the blade into my heart or my guts. Mishima had a few thousand years of philosophy behind him, and a man with a samurai sword standing next to him, ready to lop off his head. I had neither. Four years of philosophy might make you want to kill yourself, but it's not nearly enough to help you go through with it.

I left the knife on the floor, took a spindly kitchen chair—one with arms—and slid it down the hallway against the closed bedroom door. Back in the kitchen, I reached under the sink for a roll of heavy electrical tape. Then to the front room again, where I snatched my trench coat from a hook by the door. I put the coat on and slipped the belt out of the loops. I made a noose with the buckle, tied a knot in the long end of the belt, then flipped the knot over the top of the bedroom door. I closed the door, tugged on the belt, and saw immediately that it could hold my weight, no problem.

Now instead of her having stabbed me, it would look as if she'd followed me home (I was still wearing my trench coat, after all), then strapped me to the chair with the electrical tape before strangling me with the belt. She was a big woman, this student of mine—they'd see that when they arrested her. Big and crazy. She'd overpowered me, bound me to the chair, made a noose out of the belt, looped it over the door, and let me strangle to death.

I had to admit that this was my best plan ever. In my mania, I had even forgotten about the "killing myself" part of the setup, having centered most of my scheme around the idea of framing this poor, lonely woman.

The first problem, I soon discovered, was taping myself to the chair.

The feet were simple as pie. Just put each foot next to one of the front chair legs, and wrap the tape tight around the ankles. And the right hand was no problem, either— just get the tape started, roll it around the wrist and arm a few times, then bend down and rip the tape off with my teeth.

It was the left hand that would be tricky. I was right-handed, and had already taped that arm to the chair.

With my free left hand, I stuck the exposed end of the tape to the left arm of the chair, wrapped it around a couple of times loosely, bit it off, then worked my hand the best I could through the loop. It was pretty sloppy, not in the least convincing, but it would do for show.

The belt noose was hanging a few inches above and behind my head, flush against the bedroom door. I raised myself and the chair off the ground, sliding up against the closed door, trying to nudge the noose around to my face so I could fit my chin through the hole. Eventually, using my nose and mouth, I got it into position. Then, with the noose around my neck, I paused to catch my breath.

I should've thought of all this beforehand.

I took a last look around at my little apartment and slowly sat back down, feeling the fabric tighten around my throat.

When I was a kid, I experimented a lot with cutting off the blood flow to my brain, to see how close I could get to passing out. I'd use my sister's jump ropes or hang my head over the back of a chair. I always stopped before the lights went out completely.

It was the same old feeling here. First the lips begin to feel cold and thick, and the ears begin to ring a little. Then the eyes feel as if they're going to pop out of their sockets, but the lids swell and close up, I guess to keep the eyes in place. The ringing in the ears gets louder and louder, blocking out all other sounds, and the head starts to pound. Soon everything goes red.

Now, though, something was wrong.

It wasn't happening fast enough. The blood was pounding in my head, and my breathing was labored, but I wasn't flying toward unconsciousness the way I used to when I was young. I'd been hanging there for what seemed ten or fifteen minutes, and I was still every bit as conscious as when I started. Except now I had a headache and I couldn't hear anything around the ringing.

I dangled with my butt inches above the seat of the chair for some minutes more, hoping it would surprise me, sneak up on me, slap me into darkness. It didn't.

This time it wasn't a matter of losing my nerve—it was a question of realizing that my plan simply would not work. I tore my left hand from the loose loop of tape (*That wouldn't've fooled anybody anyway*) and started freeing my right wrist. Doing so, however, pulled my body around, twisted the chair a few inches from the door, and tightened the noose around my neck. Things started going dark.

My fingers clawed at the tape around my right arm. *No! This can't happen!* I could feel myself slipping—much too quickly—into unconsciousness. *Not now!*

As I grunted with the effort, my right hand twisted from the chair, and both hands shot to my neck. I pulled the belt away from my esophagus and jugular. I took a raspy, desperate breath of air, and removed the noose from around my aching head.

Freed, mostly, I sat back and thought about what I'd just done, what I'd just tried to do.

That was really fucking stupid. Really, REALLY fucking stupid.

I leaned over to untape my legs, realizing how dumb I looked. That woman would've continued to walk the streets freely. Frustrated and exhausted, more depressed than ever, I put everything away, poured myself half a milk glass of whiskey, downed it, and went to bed.

The next morning I got up, put on my trench coat, and wandered downtown, stopping in every drugstore I passed, lifting as many boxes of over-the-counter sleeping pills as I could fit into my deep pockets. Dozens of packages, over three separate trips. That night, all hesitation flushed from my muscles, the shirt with the knife rips still on my back, the flimsy steak knife still lying on the floor, I would wash the pills down with the bottle of cheap scotch sitting atop the refrigerator, waiting for just such an occasion.

I couldn't tell all that to my mom while I was strapped down to a hospital bed. It would break her. She knew that I'd tried such things before. She'd seen the bandages and, later, the scars from the previous time.

When you're in the moment—planning, preparing, executing, lost in the cruel logic—you cannot afford to think of the people you care most about. That would ruin everything. Afterward, when you've failed again and you are confronted with the people you could not afford to think about, only then can you look at the plan from the outside, and see what a stupid ass you've been.

There was the time—I must have been about fifteen, and had come home from school all jittery with annoying youthful enthusiasm. I'd been reading Descartes and the Transcendentalists and a bit of Indian philosophy for the first time. I sat by the back door tugging off my shoes and started explaining a theory of mine to my mom as she stood at the stove working on dinner. Nothing we saw around us, including her, including me, existed, I proposed. It was all merely a grand dream—whether it was ours or a distant god's, we'd never know. We were nothing but figments of someone or something's imagination, and therefore, nothing we did really mattered.

I went on outlining my theory, tickled and proud, until my mom finally turned from the stove and looked at me with a quiet sadness in her eyes. "You know, Jim," she said, "sometimes you make me real mad."

With that, I fell silent with shame and went up to my room feeling like a show-off. She was a smart and sensible woman, my mother, but she simply had no time for cocka-mamie half-baked adolescent philosophy. She knew already that it would lead to nothing but trouble. Sometimes I think she was right. Sometimes I think I would have done a much better job of getting along in the world had I listened to her and not taken my own nonexistence so seriously.

"Let's talk about it later," I told her now, referring to the pills. "Once I'm out of this place."

So much else has happened between then and now— events I didn't know how to tell anyone about. Not until I understood them more clearly myself.

2. *eins*

War had been declared that morning. I couldn't remember who was fighting whom, or where, or what had set it off. It didn't matter. I had dropped out of everything the previous day, and didn't care about what was happening across the hall, let alone on the other side of the world. I slid the phone bill and the electric bill into the mailbox, and then I dropped out. More than the hippies did, though, I was going to take that one extra step that mattered. I didn't go to class, didn't call in sick, spoke not a word to anyone.

That night, I didn't turn on the news as I normally would have. Instead, I sat at my desk and methodically punctured foil packets and dropped pill after pill into the styrofoam cup in front of me. Most were green and blue. A few yellow ones, a few pink. Soft pastel colors to bring solace and calm to the troubled psyche.

When I had emptied all the packets and dumped them into the trashcan next to my desk, I emptied that garbage into a large black plastic bag. Then I went back into my bedroom, gathered the evidence that could've pinned any number of minor crimes on me—the mail that wasn't mine, a few other things I had stolen—and took the whole mess out to the dumpster behind the building. I wasn't embarrassed about any of these crimes, I simply didn't want investigators interrogating my parents about them. They didn't need to deal with that on top of everything else.

I didn't believe in spirits, but what was happening to me was, again, most definitely the work of a bad spirit. A Bitter Angel led me into the kitchen to grab the bottle of scotch from on top of the refrigerator. Spirits were my excuse, a convenient metaphor I'd come to rely on. I'd done this sort of thing before, yet in every instance it was as if I was being pushed along by some external force. It was easier than taking responsibility for my own actions.

In the front room, I sat cross-legged on the wooden floor—on the spot where I'd sat with the knife the night before—and stared at the bottle and the cup of pills in front of me.

I screwed the top off the bottle and poured scotch into the styrofoam cup, nearly filling it before I realized what a mistake that was. Four or five pills floated to the surface, but the rest remained stuck to the bottom of the cup, melting into a gritty, colorful mess. In a panic, I gulped the scotch and a few of the floating pills. It was bad scotch to begin with, now made even more bitter with chemicals and imminent death. I gagged once, but held the bile down. I reached my fingers into the cup and scraped out what I could from the dissolving paste at the bottom before ramming it deep down my throat. The goo coated my lips and tongue. Again. Again. Again. I took hits from the bottle to wash the grit off my teeth. Then I would reach into the cup again.

My lips and tongue went numb first.

It worked more quickly than I had expected. Much more quickly than the noose. Within a few minutes, I was forgetting things. Then everything went black, the room reappearing only in flashes. I remember trying to crawl toward the front door on my hands and knees, my arms trembling violently with the effort, unable to hold the weight of my body off the ground. I raised myself on my shaking arms, then collapsed. The door was locked, the knob too far off the ground for me to reach.

There was darkness, then a flash of white.

One of the cops—there were three of them in all—had me by the shoulders and was slamming me against the wall in the hallway outside my apartment. Soon the three joined into one giant Cop with a hundred hands and two dozen moustaches.

"*Wha'd ya take?*" he growled.

Slam.

"No-Doz and coffee——" I started to lie.

Slam.

"Wha'd ya *take?*"

The Big Cop pushed me back through the doorway, back into my apartment, where I tripped backward over the ugly, squat kidney-shaped table in the middle of the room. I didn't hear myself crash and slump on the wooden floor. He smelled like vomit and gin. I watched the door slam shut behind him and felt the first boot land in my gut—

"Wha'd ya *take?*"

The Big Cop divided into three again. One part of him cleared off the top of my desk, the phone falling a few inches from my ear, the receiver humming helplessly. Another part of him went into the bedroom, and I heard the sound of a toppling bookshelf as the boot landed deep in my gut once more—

"Wha'd ya *take?*"

Then I saw him, for the first time. The front door was open again, and he was in the hall, behind the cop who was kicking me. Bald head. Mottled skin pulled tight and burned shiny onto the skull. His eyes shone like black fire. Hanging on a wrought-iron staircase behind the small crowd of neighbors who had gathered to watch the beating. He was laughing. I broke free from the Big Cop, stood, and ran. I knew I had to catch him, if only to get him out of the building. And maybe if I caught him, the cops would leave me alone.

When I stumbled out the doorway and through the cluster of neighbors, he was waiting for me at the end of the hall.

As I started toward him, he grasped the stair railing and like a gymnast swung himself around and dismounted, then headed downstairs to the basement. There was nothing down there but a clean, bright hallway and a laundry room. He would be trapped, and if I could evade the cops for just a few more minutes—*just a few more minutes*—only long enough to grab hold of Satan, or whichever of his demons this was, all my troubles would be over.

When I reached the bottom of the stairs, however, it wasn't the basement of my building anymore. At least not the one I remembered. It looked like the inside of a steel mill, full of ancient machinery that towered above me, a place of deep shadows and open flames. Pistons churned and squealed in the firelit darkness.

There he was again—shirt glued to his body, dirty black pants—above me, then behind, leaping from machine to machine with the agility of an insect. I tried to follow. Outside the building, onto a fire escape. He was waiting there, still laughing, waiting for me to grab him. I reached out my hand—my arms weren't trembling anymore—before being pulled back through a window into the hallway by the Big Cop. I tried to take a few steps forward and heard the door slam beside me. It was chilly.

What happened to my shirt?

I was in the back of a police cruiser, shirtless and shivering in the cold Minneapolis November air. The heavy mesh screen before my eyes, which separated the front seat from the back, quivered like a spider's web in a light rain. The Big Cop had split again into three figures—two in the front, one in back with me. My hands were tightly cuffed behind me. My shoulders and ribs ached.

Everything had seemed so simple earlier that day when I walked from drugstore to drugstore, filling my pockets with packages of sleeping pills. Now, trapped in the back of the squad car, I was into something I could no longer control. There was no more question of giving up.

EXAMINATION
Intern's Notes [handwritten, unsigned]

22 w.m. brought in by MPD after being found by apt. manager wandering the halls in confusion.

Problem
Suicide attempt. 10.85 wrist slashing. But claims other suicide attempts also.

Myopia. Night blindness.

CT scan done after walking into a pole several months ago.

"I looked into the sun as a child, because I was told not to."

Confused on many details not substantiated.

Conversation with mother—he thinks his grandmother died yesterday, and that he saw his whole family at that time, however he hasn't seen his parents in two months.

Unsure of city he's in—"Is this still Minneapolis?"

Thought that people were walking through walls, "like ghosts" in the ER.

He claims he's always had disjointed thoughts.

He claims 7 days ago he also walked into a pole at night and that he is troubled by vertigo and has trouble walking.

Tonight he is confused as to what happened, but claims he drank one beer, took 4 No-Doz and some aspirin, denies other drugs or attempted suicide. However, he claims he "feels suicidal every day," and besides the cut wrists has also tried "hanging," "drinking chemicals," "throwing myself down stairs."

The patient is a university student working on a PhD under stress lately. 4 weeks of the quarter left, 3 seminar papers due, also working on a paper on schizophrenia and grading tests.

3 · I See You

"It works," she explained. "It sucks up the poison just fine. But it's always hell to clean out afterwards. It plugs everything up. Now roll over on your left side."

The day nurse during my stay in intensive care made the ordeal of lying in a hard bed, without being able to sit up, to turn over or move around freely, much easier. She brought me sodas with long straws, gave me sponge baths, and even washed my hair once. She had black hair that fell in unkempt bangs, kind eyes, and a sense of humor, even when she had to give me an enema after nothing else would loosen the solid clog in my bowels caused by a noxious charcoal drink I was given upon arrival at the hospital.

After a few days of reasonable calm on my part, a few days during which I didn't scream or rhyme or thrash about, the hospital staff left the leather straps off me when I slept. The tubes and wires spiraling away from my body held me in place just fine; I had stopped trying to rip them out. I no longer seemed to be a serious threat to others or myself. And I wasn't. At least I didn't feel like one.

Taking the step, making the final decision to try to destroy myself, then actually doing something—however slight, stupid, or devastating—had purged all the bad spirits from my head. I wouldn't even think about it again for a year or so. I felt clean, refreshed, and strong, despite my circumstances. I was happy to be alive. Everything was fine. I'd wait it out in the ICU for a few days, until my kidneys cleared up, then get moved to a regular room for a few more days, to make sure everything was in place and functioning as it should, then go home and back to work.

That's the way I figured it.

I was in the ICU for a week and a half. Doctors, several of them, stopped by daily to see if my kidneys were operating at full capacity yet.

"We thought we lost you there for a while," the first doctor told me. He was a younger fellow, name of Tomlinson, and he was in charge of my case.

"You did," I replied. "That was the whole idea." I stopped short of going on to tell him about the various places I had been before I arrived at the hospital. There was no point. I'd let the doctors take care of my body, then send me on my way.

Med students stopped by a few times, to practice their bedside manner. When one of them worked up the courage to ask me why I'd done it, I gave him my established answer, explaining as plainly as I could that it was a simple, heartfelt reaction against the boredom, against the ceaseless repetition everyone had to live with every day.

I was no longer able to walk home from the liquor store or buy groceries or cook dinner without being aware of what I was doing in an acute, physically painful sense. I'm not sure he understood what I was trying to get at. I didn't push it. I let him and the others think they had done a good job of lifting my spirits. Normally they would have annoyed me, but in intensive care I was glad to have the company.

I was like a crippled yogi of despair. From my perspective, seeing their bright, eager, still uncynical eyes staring at me from the bedside, as they waited anxiously for my answers to their questions, I was doing them a favor, giving them something they might mull over, as opposed something they would expect. It seemed a nice thing to do.

One thing I didn't tell them about was the letter I had dropped in the mail to my friend Laura the day before I pulled my stunts with the knife, then the belt.

I had met Laura in Chicago in 1983, and we'd been friends ever since, writing letters and talking on the phone. During the previous few weeks, though, it had felt as if we might become something more than that. I mentioned this in the letter, sent it off, and knew immediately there was nothing left to do. I couldn't allow myself to love anyone in that way. Simply could not do it. My only option, after leaving the letter in the box, was escape— whatever form it might assume.

I had spent too many years forging an identity for

myself—as smart-assed youngsters who see too many movies and read too many pulp novels will do—as a Man Alone. I loved my family dearly, yes, and I loved what few friends I had. But—and this is hardly a unique dilemma—this situation was different. This meant confessing to an emotion I would never admit to suffering. Doing that meant admitting I wanted someone near me. I couldn't have that. It was a sign of weakness. I would admit to no ties, nothing that could hold me down in any way: no philosophy, no religion, no politics, and certainly no love. I would gladly confess to things—as I had with the medical students—that would make other people happy, satisfy them, and then send them on their way, just as long as they would leave me alone again. All I really was asking from the world at large was to be left alone.

At least that's what I kept telling myself I wanted. That's why the letter I'd sent down to Chicago had been such a horrifying and life-ending revelation for me. For once I'd dared to glance through the murk of image with which I'd surrounded myself, and seen what rested behind it, and I didn't care to deal with its existence.

But since it was there, my job was to get rid of it.

Through reading and listening over the years, I've found that most people can justify and explain away their suicidal impulses—any impulse, in fact—with remarkable, even stunning, ease. Bad job, troubled relationship, rotten childhood, desperate money problems, petty crimes they can no longer conceal. It was never that simple for me.

I had been trying to kill myself since I was fourteen. I came from a loving family and a solid, middle-class midwestern existence. A decade later, I was working, I was getting by. I was a petty criminal and a bit of a thug, too, sure—but I'd never been caught. I had no rational excuses to offer. No matter how I had tried, nothing worked. I threw myself down flights of stairs, drank bleach, cut my wrists, stepped in front of buses, all to no avail.

The last few times, I'd attribute to boredom—not being able to escape the banal necessities of life. Balancing the checkbook. Making the bed. Cleaning the tub. Walking to the bus stop. Riding the bus. Walking home from the bus stop.

Any Freudian worth his salt, of course, would never accept an answer like that. He would argue that there was some true answer, some forgotten horror, buried deep in the unconscious that needed to be dredged to the surface.

Yeah, well, people say a lot of things. Despite my own suspicions, I was happy to stick with with the boredom explanation.

Like most everyone, when I was a youngster, I had big plans for myself. I knew early on what I wanted to be when I grew up. After seeing *Earthquake,* I wanted to be a seismologist and study the San Andreas Fault. After seeing *Jaws,* I wanted to be ichthyologist and study sharks. After sitting through all thirteen episodes of *Cosmos,* I was set: I was going to be an astronomer or a theoretical physicist. I was able to fake that last one pretty well—at least until my first two weeks of physics courses at the University of Chicago.

From my earliest "I'm going to be a seismologist" days, whichever road I took, I knew I would end up being one kind of scientist or another. Let those other kids be the firemen and the cops, the baseball players, short-order cooks, and car salesmen. Scientists in the movies always knew what the real score was. They were always ahead of the government, the military, and the press, even if nobody else believed them. Of course those great men and women of science usually died before the final reel as a result of their arcane wisdom, but I could accept that. It was the arcane wisdom itself I was after—not the adulation of the masses who'd been saved.

At the age of ten, I was gearing damn near everything I did toward becoming an ichthyologist. I paid attention to the biology and earth science sections in school. I read about fish, the ocean, shipwrecks, everything I could connect to it in any way. I saved up my allowance and bought a twenty-gallon aquarium, which I stocked with miniature eels and red-tailed sharks and hermit crabs and aquatic frogs. None of that guppy shit—guppies were boring and common. Unfortunately, each of those delicate creatures in my aquarium died a bizarre and untimely death because of my ignorance and incompetence. It was all part of the learning process, I figured.

A few years later, once I had taken the book learning as far as it would go toward my goal, it was time for the next step. If I was going to be the next Jacques Cousteau or Matt Hooper, I would have to learn how to scuba dive. For years I had stared longingly at images of men and women in rubber suits, diving masks, and Aqua-lungs, paddling slowly and blissfully through the crystal-blue waters around the Great Barrier Reef. Granted, these were the very men and women who were ofttimes mauled by sharks. Swim around underwater with sharks, you're bound to get mauled sooner or later. After you get sewn up, you dive back in and do it some more. That was all fine with me.

Scuba diving, predictably, was not the most popular sport in northeastern Wisconsin, where I grew up. At least not as long as snowmobiles and shotguns still existed. But my enthusiasm eventually convinced my parents that it was a necessary step along my planned career path. The cheap mask, snorkel, and fins I had purchased at the local Kmart for use at the public pool down the street were not sufficient anymore. My dad, who by sheer force of personality alone seemed to be acquainted with everybody and everything in Green Bay, knew a place that might be able to help me out.

Adventure Sports, it was called, and so one Saturday afternoon we drove there. Adventure Sports mainly sold camping and mountain climbing and hunting equipment, but sure enough, in a little corner in the back was a section of scuba gear. A fellow named Steve ran the place. He was a short man, who looked a bit like Dustin Hoffman with curly hair. He told us that the store offered introductory scuba classes. Six weeks long, every Wednesday night from six till ten at Southwest High, the only school in the area with an indoor pool.

My dad signed me up for the next set of classes, and I was thrilled. We picked me up some new fins and a new snorkel, and made arrangements to order a mask with my optical prescription built into the faceplate. My folks were great that way—always eager to encourage me in the things I was excited about. They were doubly eager when these things involved some kind of physical activity, me being a weak and scrawny child.

After my dad dropped me off at Southwest the first night, I discovered that fifteen people would be in the class with me. All of them were male, most in their late twenties and early thirties. I was a good decade younger than any of them. I also found that instead of being handed equipment and allowed to splash about in the pool for four hours, we would spend the first half of each session on classroom work, with a textbook, a teacher, a blackboard, and quizzes. I hated quizzes, but I was working toward a clear, obvious, attainable goal. Something I could use and something I needed. I didn't complain. I threw everything I had into my new studies.

We were taught, and expected to know, the engineering involved in the design of the self-contained underwater breathing apparatus. We learned the basics of fluid mechanics. We learned physiology, and how the lungs worked, and how oxygen behaved in the bloodstream under different pressures. We learned first aid in treating people who forgot what they had learned about how oxygen behaved in the bloodstream under different pressures, and ended up with the bends. We even learned the proper way to explore a shipwreck and what specific elements of underwater life might potentially kill us. It was all stuff the public schools would never even have considered teaching. The more I learned, the more convinced I became that this was what I wanted to do.

After two hours in the classroom, we were led out to the pool, where we were handed masks, flotation vests, fins, weight belts, and air tanks. But we didn't strap it all on and then swim around on our own, as I thought we would; we were, it turned out, in gym class. I hated gym class, too—but again, I swallowed my complaints. We had to swim laps normally, then swim using the snorkel; we had to learn how to hold our breath, and buddy-breathe, and read a variety of gauges underwater, and dive backward off a board while wearing fifty pounds of metal.

It was exhausting for a thirteen-year-old who was in no physical condition whatsoever. Despite that, despite the fact that after being in the water for fifteen minutes I was usually shivering uncontrollably, teeth chattering like castanets, despite the fact that nobody but Steve talked to me (everyone else was there with a friend or two), I kept going back. And I kept going back because, whatever the growing evidence that I was maybe not cut out for this quite yet, it was something I desperately *wanted* to be cut out for.

All it took to convince me was the third night of classes, when we were first allowed to swim freely with the tanks underwater. It was an absolutely delightful, almost magical sensation, to be flying underwater. Flying, breathing, seeing clearly, and listening to the silence of it all—silence, except for the hollow mechanical inhalation through the regulator in my mouth and the soft burbling as I exhaled. Granted, I was only in a high school swimming pool, but I was skimming around the bottom of a high school swimming pool, seeing for the first time what the bottom of a high school swimming pool looked like up close.

The final night of classes, we were given two tests. The first was a written exam in the classroom, the second a diving test. All but two people in the class (including me) failed the written test. I had never failed a test, and was devastated. So when we gathered by the pool, the two who had passed the test gloating and laughing arrogantly at the rest of us, I encouraged others to take their diving test before me, while fighting off the urge to get dressed and leave.

"No, you go next, that's okay," I kept saying. I was near tears as it was, and didn't want these older fellows to see me fail the whole shebang. They'd just laugh at me.

The test proceeded this way: Each student, fully equipped, was to dive to the deepest point in the pool, then remove all his equipment—mask, vest, fins, tank, weight belt—and return to the surface, leaving everything in a pile on the pool's floor. Then the student had to dive down to the pile and put everything back on underwater.

It sounded very simple, but for, again, a scrawny child like me, it was impossible to get to the bottom of the pool without wearing twenty pounds of lead around my waist. I just floated.

After everyone else had done it, and everyone else had passed, it was finally my turn. Getting to the bottom and removing the equipment was no problem. Returning to the surface was no problem. But then it was time to force my body back down there, with all the forces of nature working against me.

I tried once, and floated to the surface before getting very far. I dove, and rose again. Time passed. The other students showered, dressed, and went home, as I grew more and more weary, yet more and more desperate not to fail a second time in one night. Over and over I flailed helplessly at the surface, and swallowed a lot of water. For an instant I thought that if I swallowed enough I might be able to equalize my body's density with that of the surrounding pool water, thus making my job easier. This idea, like so many others, did not work.

With each attempt, I could feel myself getting closer to the bottom, though never close enough. Every time I hit the surface, I looked at the instructors on the side of the pool, glancing at their watches, their shouts of encouragement growing more halfhearted and annoyed. They knew I wasn't going to make it. *Twice in one night,* I kept thinking. *Not for something this important. I can't.*

My desperation turning to fury, I filled my lungs, bent at the waist, and lifted my matchstick legs into the air. I could feel my body sliding downward, my eyes shut tight, my arms in front of me, feeling for anything at all.

As I was about to give up and float to the surface one last time, I felt a strong hand grip my wrist and yank me deeper. I hit bottom and clamped my legs around the sunken scuba tank to hold myself in place. I found the regulator, popped it in my mouth, blew the water out, and started breathing sweet compressed air again. I felt around and found my mask, pulled it over my head, pushed the heel of my hand against the top of the faceplate, and exhaled through my nose to clear the water out. It worked. That technique had never worked for me.

Finally I opened my eyes and saw Steve, who had offered that much-needed helping hand, floating a few feet in front of me. He gave me the thumbs-up sign.

I strapped on the rest of the equipment and the two of us swam to the surface. When my head broke water, the instructors on the side of the pool cheered, and I smiled around the hunk of plastic and metal in my mouth.

Over the next two weeks, I studied the scuba-diving textbook more than I'd ever studied anything. I worked out decompression rates time and again. I memorized the textbook, while my schoolwork slid. When I knew I was ready, I made an appointment to retake the written test. This time I passed.

A few weeks later, I received my certification card in the mail. After that, I never went scuba diving again. I knew that I wouldn't always have a helping hand around underwater, should I need it. Lord knows I'd need it. Besides, at thirteen, I was quickly deciding to become an astrophysicist instead.

Now, all these years later, I was trying to become a good little academic, but finding I couldn't do that very well. And after years of trying to kill myself, I had come to the conclusion that I couldn't do that, either. I simply wasn't very good at most things. My moments of victory in life had been rare, and rarely all that sweet. In fact, my moments of victory were never mine alone. No matter how much I wanted to be independent and self-reliant, no matter how much I wanted to be a Man Alone, I always needed a helping hand, as I had in that swimming pool—someone to give me a boost at the proper time.

As I lay in the intensive care cubicle, alone much of the time, I thought about what I had tried to do, what I had actually done, and how I had failed again.

All of my suicide attempts, including this one, had been sissy moves: razors, pills, poisons of assorted kinds—insecticide, bleach. I was gutless. It felt as if I was serious, both at the time and in the weeks leading to it, when I would make my plans and replay them in my head incessantly. The fact that I'd never been able to pull it off should have told me something.

I was pissed at myself for failing again and pissed at myself for almost going too far. Because I had tried and failed again in a manner that became far more public than I had anticipated, I had to look into my parents' eyes and make some attempt to explain it to them. I'd had to do that two years earlier, in Madison, after I'd opened my veins. I'd gone home for a weekend when I was released from the psych ward there. No matter how I tried, there was no hiding the bandages or the scars. That weekend hadn't been any fun at all.

I didn't just have to face my parents this time. I had to face a landlord who could throw me out on the streets for a stunt like this. My neighbors, too, who found me wandering the halls: they could be trouble. Then again, maybe they wouldn't be so bad—we'd always ignored one another in the past, minded our own business. It might be okay. But the landlord still had me worried. I'd seen him throw others out.

During my entire stay in the ICU, nobody mentioned psych wards to me. Nobody even implied it. It was their big punch line. I should've seen it coming as I lay thinking my stupid thoughts. Perhaps I did, but I didn't want to admit it to myself, and didn't care to ask anyone about it.

4. *z w e i*

"Drink it."

Everything around me was a calm, cold, solid white. I was half sitting on something, but I couldn't see it. I heard a voice telling me to drink. Another styrofoam cup was in my hand.

"Most people can't hold it down, but we'll try anyway."

It tasted like coffee that had brewed for a week. The sludge at the bottom was like coal dust. I was right about that part, at least.

"It's charcoal," the voice explained. "It'll soak up the poisons in your stomach."

The voice went away, leaving me to the silence and the whiteness. I found that I could move my head, and when I did, I started to see some of the things around me. It looked like an examination room, tiny and empty except for the table I was sitting on and a small wooden chair facing me from one corner. There was a clean, polished stainless-steel door with a round porthole cut into it. From

around the edges of the door came evidence of activity—
shuffling feet, muffled voices, radios, grinding metal
wheels.

It seemed to be a barren hospital room, but the little
I could see through the porthole looked dingy and dark,
like an old police precinct. Shadows of human heads
passed by the window.

The door swung open silently and a boy came in—
probably only a few years younger than I was, sixteen or
seventeen maybe. He was skinny, with long greasy hair,
and was wearing a heavy-metal T-shirt. I couldn't read
the name of the band. Whoever it was had one of those
logos that are so cartoonishly gothic that they're impossible to decipher.

He didn't say a word. Hardly looked at me. Walked
over to the chair in the corner and sat down. Still didn't say
anything, just stared with dark, baleful eyes. He was trying, and failing, to grow a mustache. His face was gaunt
and pale. I looked around, trying to avoid his gaze. I looked
out the porthole window again, only to find Gary staring
back at me.

Gary? Gary Farrell!

Gary and I had been friends since first grade in Green
Bay, but I hadn't seen him in five years, a few days before
I left for Chicago. I was leaving for college, and he was
about to get married and join the Navy. And now he was
here in Minneapolis? It didn't make sense.

His eyes filled with malice as he looked me up and

down through the window. He hated what he saw, what I had become, and wanted nothing to do with it. He didn't open the door.

His face vanished.

A minute later, the door opened a crack and a tiny black kitten scampered into the room and disappeared under the bed.

The voice that had told me to drink the charcoal returned as well, this time with a body attached. It talked but I was no longer listening. It didn't seem to notice the kid in the chair, and if it did, it didn't care about him. Fortunately, it didn't notice the kitten, either. I caught another glimpse of the kitten out of the corner of my eye as it slipped out from under the bed and wandered behind the legs of the voice. Around the chair, along the wall, back toward the bed. If it was found, I knew, it would be killed.

But the voice still didn't notice, and once it was clear to me that the kitten was safe under the bed, I began to listen to what the voice was saying. The last words I heard it speak were:

"And so now you're going on a bus."

Two men in white strapped me down onto a stretcher that was only six inches off the ground, and wheeled me out the door and through the precinct. I recognized half the faces that I saw from my vantage point just above the floor—old neighbors, relatives I hadn't seen since I was ten, girls I'd once tried to date.

I was crammed into the very back of an already horribly overcrowded city bus, wedged tightly behind a mass of commuters reading papers and holding children, obviously annoyed by the inconvenience I presented. I tried to apologize, but the words wouldn't come out. The bus wheezed away from the curb. It was night, and the lights of the city flashed by the windows. I wasn't in much of a position to look out the windows to see where we were going, as my head was tilted toward the floor. All I could do was read the advertisements above the windows.

Foot Doctor.

Job Skills.

Pregnancy Counselor.

My face.

Cure Drug Addiction.

I went back to the one with my face on it.

"Missing child," it read. "Have you seen him? $2,500 reward for information leading to his recovery."

I wormed one of my arms free from its strap and tugged on the pant leg of a man sitting next to me. He looked down from his paper at me with undisguised disgust. Still unable to speak, I pointed toward the sign with my face on it. He looked at the sign, then at me. Then at the sign again.

"Hey—hey!" he said, dropping his paper and pulling himself up the crowded aisle toward the driver. "It's the

lost kid! The lost kid's right here on this bus! Hey!
Driver!"

Curious eyes directed their gaze to me. A few looked
up at the sign and back to me. A few more rose from their
seats and moved toward the rear of the bus.

I kept gesturing toward the sign and then toward my
face.

More voices were raised—

"It's him!"

"Not that lost boy!"

"It's *him*!"

The driver stopped the bus and stepped through the
crowd, then leaned down close to scrutinize my face.

"Yeah, it's him, all right—I gotta call this in."

The other passengers broke out in a cheer.

"We have the lost kid right here," the driver radioed
to his station, "and we're bringing him in!"

The passengers cheered again. If I had seen this in a
movie, I would've been embarrassed for the actors. As it
was, I was embarrassed only for myself—and the fact that
all these people would have to divide up a measly $2,500
reward.

The bus drove farther, much longer than I had expected. The cheers eventually died down. After another
half-hour, I heard a police escort, sirens howling, arrive on
either side of the bus. In a few minutes it was obvious
that we were pulling in someplace. I craned my neck up
against the restraining straps just in time to see that we

were entering a cavernous gray garage, poorly lit, full of other city buses.

With a dying hiss of the air brakes, the door opened, and another cheer resounded from outside the bus. Apparently word had spread.

After being pried from the back of the bus by two men with crowbars, I was blasted through a pair of swinging doors into another blinding-white room.

Everything slowed to a halt. This time it was pretty clear that I was in a hospital. I was left in a hallway, alone, next to a wall. There were a number of other stretchers in the hallway, all empty. It was careless, given my new celebrity status. How could I have been forgotten so quickly?

Then I heard the laughter. A low, dry chuckle.

I looked to my right, across the hall, and there lay Satan—his face burned, his eyes wild, his crooked-tooth smile as wicked as it had been back at my apartment. He was lying on another stretcher, propped up on one elbow. I knew then what had happened. I'd died. I hadn't failed this time—I'd finally *died*—and I was in Hell.

Funny, but it didn't worry me all that much. There were no fiery pits, no blankets of worms, no pitchforks, no echoed screams of tormented souls. It was just quiet and empty and well lit. More like Sartre's hell than King James's.

A pair of invisible hands started pushing me down a

hallway. There were no doors in the hall. And it wasn't just one hall, but an infinite collection of intersecting doorless hallways—and everything was white. Floor, walls, ceiling. No landmarks to determine how far you'd traveled except for television monitors hung like security cameras at each intersection, and fluorescent lights in the ceiling. I closed my eyes and waited.

In the dim light someone thrust something to my lips. More of that vile black charcoal drink. I got it down once, but wouldn't do it again.

"No," I croaked out, turning my head away. I may have been in Hell, but that didn't mean I had to cooperate.

"Drink it." It was a female voice.

"No, it's black and foul."

"It's not black. It's just water."

I looked into the styrofoam cup in front of me, and what I saw was black, black as tar, clouded with gray.

"It's black. I won't."

"It's ice chips. You need to drink something. Take some to your lips and see."

She touched bits of ice to my lips. The ice was still black, but as it melted into my mouth, it didn't taste like charcoal. It was sweet and cold. I suddenly realized that I was very thirsty.

"Okay," I said through lips that were cracked and dry. Then everything went dark again.

Professional Diagnosis: Toxic Encephalopathy
Nearest Relative: Refuses
Date: 11.7.87   22:34

Principal Diagnosis
   Organic Intoxication
   Diphenhydramine Overdose
   Suicide Attempt

Clinical Summary
   The patient is to be transferred to MGMC Psychiatric Service on 11/15/87. . . .
   Mental status examination revealed that he did very well in memory, serial 7's, calculations and current events, with a wide vocabulary and appropriate interpretations of proverbs. His attention span was brief, and he did seem nervous, and at times seemed to be picking at things and seeing things that were not there. . . .
   Psychiatry evaluated the patient during his stay in the intensive care unit, and felt that he merited an inpatient stay on the psychiatric ward in order to arrange further attention. . . .

5 · Jessica Hahn

"Ya see that Jessica Hahn in *Playboy*?" asked the nurse who showed up with a wheelchair on the day I was to be released from the ICU.

"I can't say as I caught that, no ma'am," I told her as I settled in. She was tall and wide, with a flat nose and lifeless brown eyes. Her dirty-blond hair was cut short. Her question was snorted at me between moist chomps of gum as she helped me out of the bed and into the chair.

My back was killing me, my ass was sore, and after I'd been lying down for so long, not using my legs or arms in any normal fashion, my muscles had gone all limp. It felt good to sit upright, despite the pain. It would take a while before I'd be able to walk like a human being again. I turned my arms over and glanced at them. After the IVs and the daily blood tests, I looked like a junkie.

It became obvious almost immediately that the nurse wasn't wheeling me down to the front desk to check out. My parents, I had a feeling, wouldn't be waiting in the parking lot for me, the car engine idling, ready to speed me back to my place at 19th and Nicollet. No, when all she said when she showed up with the chair was, "We're moving you downstairs," before she started talking about *Playboy*, I knew she wasn't taking me anyplace nice.

"One of the girls showed it around," she continued. "Her boyfriend's a subscriber. I tell ya, I wouldn't put up with that with *my* boyfriend, y'know?"

"Sure."

"I don't know why she's even in that magazine. She's not pretty, and she's got these flabby boobs. They wanted flabby boobs, they should've asked *me* to be in there." She barked and cackled at her joke and cracked her gum. She wheeled me down the hallway, past the other ICU cubicles, and around a few corners until we reached a bank of elevators. She hit the down button, and we waited. Seeing that I wasn't nearly as enthusiastic about Jessica Hahn as she was, she stopped talking.

When the doors opened, she wheeled me inside. Then she pulled out a set of keys and twisted one in a lock at the bottom of the panel of buttons.

"We're going about six levels underground," she explained.

Why do people say enigmatic things like that— especially in a setting like this?

I felt the paranoia creep in, yet there was nothing I could do. I wasn't strapped into the chair, but I knew that if I tried to run, she'd be on me in a second and hurt me bad.

After the doors slid shut, the elevator didn't seem to move at all, but the numbers above the door changed. Though I tried not to think about it, I couldn't stop myself. Circle VI: The Heretics.

In *The Divine Comedy*, Dante defined heretics as "the consciously defiant." Well, I guess I was that much. I'd been eking out a career as a petty vandal and criminal as well as a graduate student.

Thing was, yes, I'd had a lot of adventures on the outside, stealing and drinking and fighting—but those adventures were penny-ante rebellions that never added up to much. There simply wasn't any adventure left in these adventures anymore, nothing unknown or unexpected, except in rare instances.

A moment later the elevator doors opened. The lights weren't as bright on this floor. There didn't seem to be any life around, either—no movement, no voices, hardly any sound except for the soft rolling of the wheelchair and the nurse's padding feet.

The nurse turned a corner and pushed me down another long hallway to a set of heavy double doors, painted red. I was surprised not to see "Abandon All Hope . . ." carved into the wall above them.

It probably was there when this place was built. Until somebody painted over it.

I knew where I had been taken.

There were no markings, no signs, no indication at all that this was the Bin. Just a red-and-white plastic sign that read "Ring for Entry" on the wall, beneath a white telephone. I'm not sure what I was expecting. Maybe a pleasant mural of some kind to keep the place as well disguised as possible.

The nurse told me to get out of the chair and wait while she had us buzzed in. I pushed myself up slowly, holding on to one of the arms just in case I couldn't support the weight. Weak and powerless. Not the best condition to be in when you're about to step across the border.

The nurse picked up the telephone receiver and announced my arrival.

Actually, it wasn't that formal and pleasant. What she did was pick up the phone, wait a moment, then say, "Got a new one for ya." She paused again, still holding the phone, and a second later the doors emitted a sharp buzz and a click. She hung up and pulled one of the doors open.

Inside, sitting on a small, ratty floral-patterned couch against the wall to my right, was a woman in her fifties, maybe older; it was hard to tell.

I also couldn't tell whether she was waiting patiently there for a visitor, or a chance to escape, though she didn't make a move as we entered. If she had been hired as a greeter, she was doing a pretty crappy job of it. She never even turned to look when the door opened.

Her thin white hair pointed every which way out of her head, and her face was a smudged and sad mess of mascara and lipstick. It looked as if the ward beautician

was on vacation that week, and this lady had been allowed
to apply her own makeup without the aid of a mirror. It
was spread around only vaguely near where it was supposed to be. She looked like a clown who would brighten
no child's birthday party.

I stepped quietly past her, keeping as much distance as
I could, ready to dodge a grasping bony hand. In my arms
I clutched a small bag my parents had brought me a week
earlier, in anticipation of my eventual release. Along with
a few clothes, they'd brought a book I'd asked for, and
some toiletries to ease the stay in intensive care. I never
bothered to look at the book, and never found a reason to
comb my hair.

I was still wearing a wrinkled blue-and-white gown
like the one the hospital had issued me upon admission. I
didn't remember putting it on, but I was wearing it when
I woke up.

Across from the couch was a door that led to the
nurses' station. Fifteen feet inside the doors I had come
through, a bright room opened up. Before I had a chance
to take it in, the nurse who had delivered me to my latest
fate handed my chart to a middle-aged woman in a beige
pantsuit who was waiting for us. She had peculiar features: her eyebrows had been plucked almost completely
away, her mouth little more than a paper cut. Everything
about her appearance struck me as sharp and cold, but she
was at least making an effort to appear gentle and sweet.

She took the chart and thanked the nurse. Without a word to me, the wheeling nurse spun the chair and waited to be buzzed out into the real world. I looked at her and knew that she was heading once again to a place where her observations about naked celebrities would be appreciated.

"I'm Ms. Cartwright," the woman in the pantsuit said, holding out a dry, thin hand. I shook it. "I'm a social worker here. I'm going to help you get settled in, Mr. . . . ?"

She looked down at the chart, her eyes puzzling over the name. I wondered briefly what she would do if I gave her a fake name just for fun, but decided against it. Neck-deep in shit here as I was, I would probably be smart to try to keep whatever footing I had. I'd play it cool for a bit.

"K-*nip*-fel," I said, pronouncing all three syllables slowly. "Jim Knipfel."

"Well, then, Jim, let me show you around." She turned, and I followed.

First was the enormous common room. Huge picture windows looked out on an almost pastoral scene. It *was* pastoral, or would have been if it hadn't been November. Although we were in Minneapolis, no snow had fallen yet that year, so the view was filled with brown grass and dead trees and empty flower beds, until you hit the huge white expanse of the Hubert H. Humphrey Metrodome about half a mile away.

It took a moment for the problem with that to strike home.

How could a place six levels underground look out onto the Metrodome? Was this a cruel joke to play on the insane? Or was I looking at an extremely realistic painted backdrop?

"Um, Ms. Carmichael?" I paused, staring out the windows.

"Cartwright."

"Cartwright, I'm sorry. . . . What's the deal with this?" I pointed toward the Metrodome.

"What do you mean?" she asked, with worried suspicion in her voice: as if I was already onto something I shouldn't be.

"The nurse who brought me down here told me we were going six levels underground. I watched the numbers on the elevator."

"And that we are—six levels beneath street level, that is. That out there is the result of some very clever landscaping."

"Uh-huh," I said, but didn't move. I continued to look out the windows, trying to wrap my brain around the idea. "I still don't get it," I finally admitted.

"Oh," she said, chuckling, "I see what you mean."

Well, thank God for that.

"The hospital was built on a hillside, so there are only a few levels of the complex that are actually *above* street

level. The rest are . . . underground. We're on the back side
of the building. That's how come we have this nice view.
Does that make sense?"

"Oh, okay. Yeah."

She led me through the common room. The checker-
board tile floor was scattered with folding tables and
molded plastic chairs. It reminded me of a school cafeteria. Here, though, there were no thick unrecognizable
odors in the air, no stains on the floor or whoops of youthful exuberance. It was almost as peaceable as the hallway
outside.

To the right was a windowed television room, fur-
nished with tattered yet plush couches and armchairs.
Several large men, eyes blank, sat in there, staring up at a
television that hung from the ceiling. Behind me, facing
the picture windows and the trees, was a long desk, the
nurses' station, where a few of my new fellow inmates
were lined up—I guessed, from having seen enough
movies—to get their pills.

Maybe cigarettes, too, from the look of them.

Almost everyone in the room was smoking. There
were one or two dirty black plastic ashtrays on each folding table, and most of them needed emptying.

Ms. Cartwright led me around a corner into a long
hallway. It was lined on both sides with closed and unmarked wooden doors. She stopped at the third door on
the right and opened it.

"This is where you'll be staying for a while." She smiled as warmly as that mouth could manage, as if showing me to a hotel suite at some fine resort.

There were two beds. It seemed someone already had dibs on the one closer to the window.

"Your roommate's name is Joey," she said after noticing that my eyes had focused on the rumpled sheets of the far bed. "You should be meeting him soon. Now, let's see what you have in your bag."

I emptied it onto a counter next to her and she started sorting through things, looking for contraband. As she felt through my clothes and examined my deodorant stick to make sure I wasn't hiding anything, she started in with the small talk. Something about her attitude shifted slightly once the door had swung shut behind us. She became more officious. In the main room, there were orderlies and other nurses, people who would come to her aid should she need it. Here, in a closed room with a crazy man, she had to be on her guard.

"What do you do for a living?" Her interest was poorly feigned.

"I'm a graduate student at the U of M. Philosophy. I teach there, too, a few classes."

"Oh." She forced another weak smile and nodded. "Do you know why you're here now?" Her voice went singsong, as if she'd discovered she was talking to a three-year-old, albeit a potentially dangerous one.

"Probably because I washed down a whole bunch of pills with a whole bunch of cheap scotch?" I smirked out of my own nervousness. "I gotta say, though, it sort of caught me by surprise, finding myself here. I mean, it happened a while ago."

She kept sorting through my few belongings, and didn't look up.

"I'm feeling much better now. Really. That's the way it works with me. I'm just fine now." She glanced up at that, then looked away.

"Do you smoke?" she asked, as if I had said nothing at all. She'd apparently noticed that most crazy people smoked.

"Yes. Well, sort of. Not cigarettes. Just cigars." That was true. A year or two earlier—after I graduated from college, when I had nothing better to do with my time, I had taken to smoking Phillies Titans—monstrous, cheap, stinky rolls of tobacco. Chain-smoking them, actually. At first I only smoked them in public to annoy my fellow citizens; then I got hooked on the chest pain.

"Really?" She spit out a false chuckle. "I'm afraid we don't allow cigars in here. Just cigarettes. If you decide you want a cigarette, ask one of the nurses at the front desk. There's only the generic brand, but nobody seems to mind. You're allowed one an hour."

"Right, no big deal. That's very nice, thank you." The anger began a slow simmer in my brain.

I was being very polite. I was answering her questions in as direct a fashion as I could muster. But every time I gave her an answer—straight and honest—she only smiled weakly and nodded a little. She was responding to me as if I were lying, as if the things I was saying weren't making any sense. It wasn't me, or what I was saying, but the fact that I was a patient in a psych ward that she was responding to. My physical location was making this social worker take everything I said as incoherent schizophrenic gibberish, or an elaborate paranoid construction.

"Let's see now, I'll need your belt," she said, as she slipped it from the loops in the pair of pants I had in my bag. "And the shoelaces." My parents had brought a pair of shoes in for me, too, though I never had a chance to wear them.

"How will I keep my shoes on, then?"

"You can wear your slippers, that's okay."

"Right."

Surprisingly, she let me keep my pen. I could do all sorts of terrible things with a pen. Hell of a lot more than I could do with a fucking shoelace. Jab it into my eye; or hers. Perform an impromptu tracheotomy. The only other thing she wouldn't let me have in the room was the razor.

"We have to keep this behind the desk up front, too, with the belt and shoelaces."

This made no sense.

"But ma'am, it's an *electric* razor—"

"Our concern isn't the razor itself." She oozed calm, arrogant authority. "Our concern is this." She held up the two-foot length of black electrical cord.

"Oh."

"You can go and ask for it whenever you want to shave."

"Okay."

"Now, before we go any further, I'd like to go over your rights. It's something we have to do—but it should only take a minute." I was certainly glad to hear that I had some rights in this place. I was mildly concerned, however, by the fact that they would take only a minute to go over.

"That's fine," I said. I was still trying to appear cheerful and cooperative and polite, but it was becoming more exhausting.

"Take a seat on the bed, I'll be right back. While you're waiting, if you could take your shoelaces out, please."

She left the room, and I sat down and started pulling the laces out of my shoes. I'd been through this routine before, in the little psych ward in Madison. They'll ask me a few stock questions to make sure I'm coherent and I know where I am, then tell me that they have the right to go through my mail. As if I'd be here long enough for anyone to send me mail. As if I'd be here long enough for anyone to even know I was here.

I looked back to the counter where my things were scattered, and saw the clipboard with my chart on it.

Hmmm . . .

As I was standing to take a peek, the door swung open. Ms. Cartwright—or was it Carmichael? Christ, I'd forgotten already—was back, more paperwork in her hands.

I sat back down.

She sat on my roommate's bed, across from me. Our knees nearly touched. I moved my legs to the right, away from her.

I grew more uncomfortable. I was still hating this woman for, as I saw it, looking at me with contempt. With her just a few inches away, though, I could sense her fear and anxiety. Part of me was glad of that—I wanted her to be frightened of me. That would balance things a bit. But another part, the nice part, wanted to tell her that it was okay, that I really wasn't anything to be afraid of, so long as she treated me normally. I guess I did want to try to make some human contact, even if it was with this woman. I hadn't had much of that lately, except with the nurse who washed my hair in the ICU. I was all alone here, and I didn't know what the hell was going on. I just wanted someone to tell me things would be fine, that *I* was fine, that I would be out of here in a jiffy. I was about to ask her first name, when she cracked the spell.

"Here, these are for you," she said without looking me in the eye. She handed me two sets of several stapled sheets. The first set of pages was headed "Patient Rights." A quick flip through revealed a mishmash of convoluted legal jargon, most of it underlined. The other set was titled "Guidelines for Oral Discussion of Patient Rights." This one appeared to contain everything that was in the first set, but in a language so simplified that even a madman could understand it.

"Before we start with this," she said, "I need to ask you a few questions."

"It's Friday," I replied, "and the president's name is Ronald Reagan."

"Those are certainly two of them. Do you care to guess the others as well?" She was not amused in the least that I was trying to make her job easier.

"No, that's okay. Why don't I just let you ask them?"

"Good."

Whenever I try to make things easier for someone, whenever I try to lighten a potentially grim scene, I end up overstepping my bounds. My intentions are misunderstood, and I'm dug in deeper. It has happened at school, at work, in my everyday dealings with people, whenever I open my mouth. I should've known better than to try that stunt in a madhouse. I could sense the shit rising past my chin.

Play it cool, dumbass, I told myself.

She reached out her hand unexpectedly, grabbed my right arm—which was mostly exposed by the hospital robe—turned it over and stared darkly at the pale skin.

"What's all that?"

I looked down, knowing exactly what she was talking

about. The flesh of both my inner arms was peppered with needle tracks. *Oh, Lord have mercy, now she's thinking I'm an addict, on top of everything else.* I've been a lot of bad things in this world, but I've never been a junkie.

"I've spent the last ten days in the ICU," I told her as calmly as I could. "You know that. I had about seven IVs stuck into me, and they took blood samples twice a day. It should be in my file there. If it's not, you can call upstairs and check it out with them."

She looked at me briefly, still holding my arm, but seemed to accept my answer.

"Of course. Now, let's see . . ." Getting on with her business, she looked over a legal pad on the clipboard. "I already asked you if you knew why you were here. And you gave me an answer." Her brow furrowed as she squinted at the page. Then she looked up at me. "Your doctor in the ICU—Dr. Tomlinson—said something else, actually."

"Really." I shrugged.

"Yes. Here he cites your 'psychotic break.' After the overdose, you suffered a psychotic break, and Dr. Tomlinson thought you should move down here so we could make sure you came out of it all right."

"First I've heard of it." I hadn't told anybody about my little adventure. Maybe it was all that rhyming I'd been doing. "What's a 'psychotic break,' anyway?" I asked.

"Well," that voice lilted again, as if she were explaining it to a slow child, "to put it simply, a psychotic break is when you lose touch with reality. Does that make sense?"

"I guess."

"It can be a temporary thing—lasting a few hours or a few days—and in your case, your doctor wanted to make sure that it was."

If it wasn't a temporary thing—if I decided to scamper away permanently—then I'd really be in trouble. Or from my perspective, no trouble at all.

"Oh. Well, yes it was," I told her. "Temporary, that is. I mean, unless of course you're a figment of my imagination." I prayed I would never have created an imaginary world as annoying and banal as this one.

She chuckled weakly again, and again I thought briefly of strangling her with my shoelaces.

"Okay . . ." She went on with her other questions: Could I count backward from a hundred by sevens, what was my address, what were my parents' names, could I explain to her what "A rolling stone gathers no moss" meant? Then she moved on to my rights.

If I did any work for the hospital while I was there, I'd be paid for it. Probably fifteen cents a day. Any mail I sent or received could be opened if it was suspected to contain contraband. Since I was not here by choice, but rather by a doctor's orders, I was free to ask a court to set me free. I was to receive "prompt and adequate treatment" to clear up my "problem." I had the right to refuse medication unless medication was deemed necessary to keep me under control. And once I was released, I could look at my records.

"Apart from all this," I asked, "what's expected of me? What do I have to do here?"

"Get better," she said vaguely, trying to be kind.

"There's no mandatory group therapy or any such nonsense?"

"We don't do much of that here. Only if the doctor thinks it necessary."

That was a relief. "Will I be put on any medication?"

"Again, only if the doctor thinks it necessary. Most of our patients are already on medication when they check in."

More good news, too. "Now this doctor—a shrink, right? When do I see him?" She had started gathering her things—and my belt, shoelaces, and razor—to leave.

"You won't be seeing him for a while." She stood up. "Get settled in. Look around if you like. If you have any questions, you can ask me."

She was reaching for the doorknob. "And—I don't know if you noticed—but the patients here are free to wear street clothes. Some do, some are more comfortable in their hospital gowns. You can do what you like. We have laundry facilities here, too, you know."

"I didn't know that. Thanks." Last time I tried to go

to a laundry room, I was chasing Satan. I decided not to share that with Ms. Cartwright, who would undoubtedly jot it down on my chart the minute she escaped the room.

"Okay, if you have any more questions, you can ask for me at the nurses' desk."

"Right, uh-huh."

She left, and I set to changing into my street clothes. *Just a hospital formality. I'll be out of here in a day or two. Once that doctor sees me, once he sees for himself how together I am, I'll be out of here and back to work.* Step 1 in proving it was to get dressed like a normal person. Always start with the basics.

I sat down on the bed to pull on my pants and looked around the room carefully for the first time. The two beds were about eighteen inches apart. Approximately two feet from the foot of the beds was the counter where most of my things were still spread out. Instead of being rectangular, the countertop was trapezoidal. Likewise, the window, which looked out onto a white concrete wall, was an unbalanced trapezoid. I hadn't noticed these things with Ms. Cartwright in the room. The walls and ceiling were tilted, and didn't meet at right angles. It was architecture out of Lovecraft and Escher.

Sitting on the bed with my pants bunched at my knees, I saw it was impossible to take a full step forward in any direction, anywhere in the room. You'd kick a wall, or a dresser, or a closet, or a desk, or the other bed. And then those odd angles looming wherever you looked, setting you off balance to begin with. Did they think I'd ignore this treachery? First the underground "view," and now this? Did they think I wouldn't *notice?*

Maybe it was part of an elaborate psychotic construction I was creating for myself. Maybe that break they were talking about wasn't temporary at all. I looked around for something—anything—normal to hold on to. I saw it through the open doorway in one corner. The room may have been designed in some other dimension, but at least I had a private bathroom: I wouldn't have to deal with a communal madhouse shower.

The door behind me opened as my roommate charged inside.

Joey didn't look at me. He marched to the far side of his bed and started cleaning off the top of his nightstand, jamming everything into the drawers—deodorant, toothbrush, whatnot—hiding it all away. Apparently he had just been told he was getting a roommate himself. As unhappy as it made me, he was in an absolute fury about the prospect.

"Hello there," I said to his back, as he ripped open drawers and slammed them shut, making sure I hadn't stolen anything already. "My name's Jim. And I guess yours is Joey . . . at least that's what the lady in the suit said. Is that it? Joey? Your name, I mean?"

Silence.

"Okay, well, I guess we're, uhh, in here together, huh?"

Silence.

"Okay, then, uhhh . . . I guess since you've been using that bed, well, then, I guess I'll just take this one." I fondly patted the thin beige bedspread I was sitting on. Then I realized I hadn't pulled my pants on all the way. They were still bunched around my knees, and I was still wearing the robe. I might as well have been chewing on the lampshade or flapping my arms and clucking like a chicken when he came in.

Joey flew out the door before I could continue my introduction. I caught only the briefest glimpse of his face as he passed. Red hair; thin, scraggly mustache. Small man, probably in his thirties, maybe younger. He was shorter than I was by a few inches, and stockier. He was wearing jeans and a blue plaid shirt. Something about him told me he came from a blue-collar background. Strange, I didn't expect to find a blue-collar type in a mental institution. I thought it more an environment for the wealthy to wean themselves off cocaine or get treatment for "exhaustion"—or for the genuinely mad, who are true classless citizens. Blue-collar people, at least in the world I grew up in, were more serious, more down-to-earth, and more stable.

I pulled my pants the rest of the way up, threw on an old sweater to cover the needle tracks, folded the hospital gown, and put my things away. I poked my head in the bathroom to take a better look. Shower, good; toilet, yes, good; sink, fine. Slick dark-blue tiles on the floor. As with the rest of my new room, the walls met at strange acute and obtuse angles. Apart from that, however, it seemed normal. Then I looked at the mirror above the sink.

It was made of polished stainless steel, not glass, so it couldn't be smashed. The reflection it bounced back was warped, distorted, melting. No wonder that woman on the couch was made up the way she was. In a mirror like this, she probably seemed a vision of perfect loveliness to herself.

I stepped out of the bathroom, grabbed my book, and headed to the day room. I needed to settle myself in and get a better sense of the place, and whom I'd be spending my next day or two with. I had no place to go but nowhere, at least for a little while, so I might as well make the best of it.

Four or five people were sitting in the darkened TV room. Either they had the volume turned down or the place was soundproofed. With the door closed, I couldn't hear a peep coming from there. Nobody anywhere was making much noise. No screaming or crying, no mad howls of anguish. In fact, it was spookily quiet.

"Can't you hear the screaming all around you?" I murmured under my breath the opening lines from Werner Herzog's *Every Man for Himself and God Against All.* "The screaming that men call silence?" I flushed the memory out of my head right away.

Off in a corner, opposite the TV room, was a station-ary bike. A gaunt, unshaven man with dark hooded eyes, long nose, and stringy black hair flecked with gray was pedaling furiously. Sweat greased his cheeks and dripped from the tip of his nose. His body rocked back and forth out of rhythm with his pumping legs. He was muttering so quietly that I couldn't catch any of it. Not until I passed near him did I even notice the sound.

Except for him, and the lady with the makeup prob-lem, who was still sitting on the couch by the door, staring, most everyone seemed to be reasonably well put together. Some were playing cards, others checkers, as if they were in a barbershop in some tiny Wisconsin town.

I'd been in psych wards that looked worse.

The Bin in Madison was pretty hellish—people bang-ing their heads against the walls or crapping themselves, others screaming at all hours. That had been an open ward, where you could check yourself out whenever you wanted. This one was locked-door. There was no walking away, no deciding for yourself that you were doing fine.

You were in here because a doctor or a judge or your family said you should be here, and there was no getting out until a doctor or a judge said you could get out. You were incarcerated. Those head-bangers in Madison might've been in clearly bad shape, but what about these people? I tried to imagine what corrupt and diabolical thoughts had brought them here in the first place—and kept them here now. Who could tell what cruel and un-predictable plans they were making as they shuffled their cards and rearranged their checkers?

I was a little disturbed at how sedate and ordinary most of them appeared. Of the dozen or so seated at the tables, roughly half wore street clothes, the other half hospital gowns. Those in street clothes wore slippers or loafers. Two were distinguished-looking businessman types—graying hair, designer glasses, nice clothes. They could have been stopping off for a drink after a round of golf. These two were probably the most dangerous of the lot.

I was thinking like that social worker. She undoubtedly knew much more about the nature of the inmates here than I did. She had her reasons for treating me the way she had.

I found myself a chair next to one of the picture windows. Nobody said anything to me. There was no big welcoming hug from the lithium set. None of the nurses or orderlies smiled or waved. They were busy with patients silently streaming up to the counter to get their meds or smokes.

I determined that for each patient the nurse had to find a chart, make sure that the medicine was on schedule and/or that at least an hour had passed since the last cigarette, then find the proper pill and/or reach for the next cigarette. Those who wanted smokes had to wait for a nurse or orderly to fire it up with the disposable lighter chained to the counter like a pen in a bank.

Everything—each request, each patient—took a long time.

Sitting by the window and watching the slow train of crazies move along proved the paradoxes entailed in Einstein's theory of relativity. Time was slowing to a standstill. It had been three o'clock for well over an hour now.

Relax, I told myself, noticing that I was starting to get antsy. *You just got here, and you're here for a bit. The way to get through it is to stay calm. The way to get out is to prove that you're sane. And the way to enjoy it is to look at it all as just another adventure—like setting a building on fire or stealing a car.*

"Okay, then," I whispered—which I realize now was no way to prove my sanity—"this is all an experience. This is all something new."

Maybe that's why I wasn't that worried as I sat and looked around. It was real, it was under way now, and Lord knew if it would ever come to an end, but it was an adventure, like everything else.

At the same time, I couldn't help wondering whether it was going to be more than I had bargained for.

It didn't bother me that nobody said hello. All I needed to do was see the doctor, get his stamp of approval on my chart, and I was on my way home. It wasn't as if I was looking for any new friends. I certainly didn't see myself inviting anyone here over to my place for Thanksgiving once they were released. I opened my book and started reading.

The only book I had with me was *Écrits*, a collection of essays by the notoriously demanding French psycho-analyst Jacques Lacan. My parents had gotten it for me from my apartment the previous week. Before everything happened, I had been reading it for a seminar I was taking.

Now, here, the book seemed especially appropriate, even when I couldn't understand a goddamn thing Lacan was talking about:

"I am characterizing this agency here not by the the-oretical construction that Freud gives us in his metapsy-chology, namely, as the perception-consciousness system, but by the phenomenological essence that he recognizes as being in experience the most constant attribute of the ego, namely, *Verneinung*, the givens of which he urges us to ap-preciate in the most general index of a prejudicial inver-sion. . . ."

Yes, well.

That first day was slow and sad, despite my attempts to look at it as an adventure. In the end, I spoke to no one—not even the nurses behind the counter. I was on no medications and I smoked only cigars, which they wouldn't allow me. I had no excuse to make my way over to the counter. I sat in my chair, watched the world dribble on around me, and occasionally tried to make sense of Lacan's impenetrable prose.

Even that kept splattering against my brain like a water balloon. I went to bed early that night, without eating. There was a well-regimented and complicated protocol surrounding meals that I didn't understand yet and was afraid to ask about, so I went without. Maybe the next day I'd ask.

Maybe not.

Roommate or not—I hadn't seen Joey around since he'd gone out the door—I crawled into bed and closed my eyes. At least the bed was snug and the sheets were clean. I was asleep almost immediately.

I reached to the nightstand, put on my glasses, raised myself in the bed, and took a look around. The room was dark, but over in the bathroom, two orderlies were swabbing the blue tiles. It seemed a peculiar time to clean the bathroom. Then, as one of them hoisted his mop toward a bucket, I saw that they were swabbing up something red. I looked at the other bed and, in the light from the bathroom, could tell that it was empty.

I don't know what hour it was when I woke. I'm not even sure what noise woke me. By the time my eyes snapped open, I had forgotten.

A couple of times during the night—and this happened every night, I would discover—someone checked in all the rooms with a flashlight to make sure that every inmate was in place and asleep. When I first awoke, I thought that was all it was. Someone had already made one pass-through that night. But this second time, the light and the sound of feet shuffling about the room weren't going away. That's when I noticed the men in the bathroom.

"What the hell happened?" I was as awake as I remembered being in years.

"None of your business," one of the orderlies said as he stepped forward to block the bathroom doorway. "Go back to sleep. Everything's fine."

I sat up fully now, and swung my legs over the side of the bed.

"None of my business? Everything's *fine*? Look at what you're doing!"

"Get back in bed. Go back to sleep. This shouldn't worry you."

This was insane.

"Blood all over the goddamn bathroom floor, and it shouldn't worry me?" What had I gotten myself into? I was a dead man for sure. I had seen this movie, and I knew immediately that I was doomed. I was not supposed to see what was happening in the bathroom. And by opening my big yap, I'd revealed myself.

I knew I wouldn't get any more information out of the orderlies. They'd probably beat me with rubber hoses if I kept demanding answers. I got back in bed, as they'd instructed, and closed my eyes. I pretended to sleep until they went away. Then I did fall asleep. I've always been able to sleep through most anything. Stress, depression, bad news: rather than stay up and think about it, I'll hide from it by going to sleep, hoping my dreams will unlock the answer for me. That hasn't happened, yet.

I woke up the next morning early, about six, hoping

last night's business might've been another mild psychotic break, like an aftershock. I took a look around in the dim predawn light. Evidence of Joey's ever having set foot in that room with me had been erased. His bed was made and his drawers had been cleaned out. There was nothing left. I checked the bathroom floor. It was spotless. Not even the tiniest flake of blood left between the blue tiles. The orderlies had done a mighty thorough job and I had slept through most of it. It was obvious from the beginning that Joey disliked the idea of having a roommate, but this response of his seemed a little extreme, even for me.

I dressed and went to the nurses' station.

Now I bet they try and deny that Joey ever existed in the first place, I thought, trying to stay one step ahead of them as the idea started growing that I was being gaslighted. Gaslighted in a madhouse—what was the point of that?

The day room was still dark, and none of the other patients was up yet.

"This might be kind of awkward timing," I said to the nurse behind the counter, without mentioning Joey by name, "but I need a shave." I rubbed my thickly stubbled chin for emphasis. "Do you suppose I could get my razor? Ms. Cartwright—Carmichael—whoever—told me yesterday I could ask for it here."

"No, I'm sorry, but you can't have it, not just now." She didn't even blink.

"But it's an *electric* razor." I returned to yesterday's

hopeless argument. "What am I gonna do, *shave* my wrists?" This time it seemed to get through.

She told me to wait while she went to talk to the doctor on staff. A few minutes later he came out front with her, holding the old shoe box in which they were guarding my contraband. He was young, he looked weary, and he had an expensive haircut. He shook my hand, and introduced himself as Dr. Ford.

"Okay, you can shave," he said, a bit more sharply than I thought necessary, "but we're going to have to send an orderly in to watch you."

"You're kidding."

"No, we're *not* kidding." He didn't look much like he ever did.

"Well, fine then." What was my choice? I just wanted to shave and be done with it. I feel crappy all day if I don't shave—and I hadn't shaved in almost a week.

"We'd also like to ask you a few questions."

"Uh-huh?" *Here we go. If I saw too much, they're going to kill me. I know it. I'm going to disappear. They're going to steal my brain. It's all those weird angles in that room—*

"How well did you know Joey?" The doctor opened the interrogation slowly and simply. At least he wasn't denying that Joey existed.

"Where is he, by the way? Where'd you take him?"

"He'll be fine," he said curtly, not answering my question. "How well did you know him?"

"I didn't know him at all—we never spoke. I tried to, the one time I saw him, but he wouldn't say anything. I just got here yesterday. Last night I went to bed early, and he must've come into the room sometime after I was asleep."

"Did you hear anything last night?"

"Not until the orderlies were cleaning things up. I have no idea what happened, I sure didn't see anything, but I think I can make a fair guess."

"You didn't hear or see anything at all until that time?"

"I told you, no. I'm a heavy sleeper."

"So, Joey, now, he didn't . . . *offer* you anything, did he?"

What an odd question.

"No, uh-uh. Like I said, he never spoke to me. Not a word."

"Any other patients offer you anything?"

"Well, no, I mean, like what? You're the first people I've talked to since I've been here . . . since I was dropped off. I haven't said a word to anybody, except Ms. Cartwright, and nobody's said a word to me. I tried to talk to the orderlies last night while they were cleaning up the bathroom, but they weren't saying anything. They told me it was none of my business and that I should go back to sleep."

Dr. Ford waited for a long time, staring at me hard, still not handing the razor over, keeping it out of reach. He was trying to size up how schizo I really was before he went on.

"Okay, this is what's happening." He set the shoe box on the counter. "Someone here—one of the patients, we believe—somehow got hold of a mirror, one of those little hand-held mirrors"—he cupped his right hand and held it up to illustrate—"and smashed it. Now they're trading shards of broken mirror to other patients for cigarettes or something. We think that's how it works. Anyway, that's what Joey used."

He gave me a stern look.

"Joey's not saying anything. He might be the one who was doing it, for all we know. But we don't. Over the next few days, until we can get to the bottom of this, just keep your ears open. Please."

Why was he telling me this? I had been there less than twenty-four hours and was being conscripted to be a rat on loons. Maybe "Joey" was a test. Maybe "Joey" was an orderly playing a patient to see what I would do.

Then it came to me. I *had* seen this movie. Sam Fuller's *Shock Corridor*. A journalist desperate to win the Pulitzer Prize checks himself into a madhouse where a murder has occurred, pretending to be a patient. It's the story of a lifetime. He finds out who the killer is (an orderly, as I remember), wins the Pulitzer, and ends up completely buggy—"a catatonic, mute schizophrenic," to be exact—locked away for the rest of his life.

Well, that's just fucking great, I thought. Then I stopped myself.

I was a suicide case, not a paranoid.

A big blond kid showed up and stood next to me. I couldn't tell whether he was one of the pair who was in my room the night before. The doctor finally relented with the razor, and the kid followed me back into my room to watch me shave.

"I can see this is going to be an interesting couple of days," I said. I plugged the razor in over the bathroom sink and switched it on. The orderly stood in the doorway, leaning against the frame, bored, watching me shave.

"Yeah, whatever," he replied.

I returned the razor to the nurse at the front desk when I was finished. Satisfied that I hadn't hanged myself, she put it in the flimsy cardboard safe-deposit box and took it to the back room. I waited patiently at the desk.

"Yes?" she asked nervously when she returned, as if she sensed already that I was going to be trouble.

"I have a little problem." I realized that wasn't the best way to open a conversation here. "I'm not sure how to go about getting meals. Up in the ICU everything was just brought to me."

The tension left her features. "That's no problem." She smiled, sounding relieved that I hadn't told her about the bugs crawling around behind my eyes. "When you get a meal, it comes with a menu card that you fill out for the next one. Choose whatever you'd like. Turn that back in to us, and you're all set."

"Yes, yes, I know that," I explained. "But um, how do I go about getting that *first* one?"

"Oh. That is a problem, isn't it?"

The next leg—starvation.

She made a call to the hospital kitchen, or wherever the psych ward food came from, and arranged for a breakfast to be brought to me along with everyone else's that morning. From then on, she promised, I shouldn't have anything to worry about. "Just be sure and fill out the card," she said. I thanked her, then went back to my room to wait for sunrise.

I dozed lightly until a few minutes after eight, when I heard several sets of feet shuffling down the hallway outside my door, and some quiet voices. That was when people got up around here. Maybe they all had a wake-up call. It was a good thing to find out. I got myself together, and by eight-fifteen had opened my door and gone to the day room to join them.

Everything was exactly as it had been the previous day. The gaunt man was back to muttering on the stationary bike. The lady with the traumatic makeup was back on the couch. The two distinguished-looking gentlemen were sitting across from each other at a table, talking quietly. The room was already hazy with cigarette smoke, like an early-morning fog you know the sun will never burn away.

I looked around for a likely candidate. Rat or not, I supposed I had a mission. It didn't matter—if I was in here, I was crazy, right? Even if I knew I was sane as stone, *they* didn't know that. To them, I was just another patient. And if I was just another patient, I must be as crazy as they were. And if I was crazy, that meant I had no conception of right and wrong. At least in a legal sense. Maybe in a place like this, being a snitch was no more or less important than being a vegetarian, or an Episcopalian. At least I was hoping that was the case.

I knew that my reasoning was mighty shaky, but I chose not to think about it. I remembered that in *Kiss of Death*, the DA referred to not squealing on principle as "that hoodlum complex." And while I had been a bit of a hoodlum on the outside, being a hoodlum was no longer an option once those doors closed and these walls wrapped around me. Everything changed then.

The thing to do was to strike up a friendly conversation with someone. Then try to get him to offer me some mirror shards. I'd never done anything like this before. Not really. Who knew whether it was a single operator, or whether all of them were involved? Maybe it was a grand secret conspiracy intent on widespread mayhem.

I hadn't seen Joey out here the day before. Just that

once when he stopped by the room to make sure I wasn't poking through his things. That meant he hadn't been hiding in the room. Maybe he'd been doing his laundry, or maybe he spent his days staring at the television. It was dark in the TV room, and the sound was muffled. I glanced through the windows. Four men were sitting there, that I could see, watching cartoons. I decided to join them.

I stood up from my chair by the window, and kept an eye on everyone as I moved across the room. Maybe it was the lady with the makeup. I came to think of her as "Edna Malaise." It's easier if you have a name to put to someone. And since this was a nuthouse, who would care—who would even notice—if I made a few names up? Yeah, she was a suspicious character, all right, what with her unblinking delirium and her immobility.

I opened the door to the television room and stepped inside. It really was soundproofed in there, the walls carpeted to contain the noise. Four pasty faces stared up toward the screen. All four men were overweight. All but one were in bathrobes.

"Good morning," I greeted them.

"Shhhh," one of them said absently from a battered green couch. The others didn't say anything or acknowledge my entrance. I went and sat next to the man on the green sofa, trying to ignore the overpowering stench of sweat and smoke that rolled off him. He had tiny piggy eyes and looked as if he might've been a child molester.

I glanced at the screen. "Cartoons, huh?"

"*Shhhh,*" the man repeated. It wasn't a good cartoon. It was an awful series, maybe *The Smurfs,* or worse, a *Smurfs* knock-off. My new friends chuckled at the mild on-screen high jinks, and laughed openly and hard at the commercials.

Maybe they're all ad execs who cracked one day.

This was getting me nowhere. I couldn't very well ask questions if I wasn't allowed to talk. I'd try them again later. Maybe these fellows were less attentive during the news. I'd return to the day room, see what I could find out there. The breakfast cart, I hoped, would arrive soon. I hadn't eaten in almost twenty-four hours, and my thinking was less than razor-sharp. Maybe I should have something in my belly before I took this business any further. I stood to leave.

When I opened the door, a voice behind me said quietly, "Bye." I turned to look. Almost hidden in the shadowed corner, a man in a chair was waving at me.

"Good-bye," I said, and gave a little wave back.

"*Shhhh,*" the man on the green couch repeated, annoyed at all the incessant jabbering.

In the day room, I returned to my seat by the window and waited for breakfast to show up. I adored hospital food. Everything had a texture and a flavor that I found comforting. It was all pillow-soft. Never any edges or bones to cut up your gums. Every item, even the meats and the vegetables, seemed to have been concocted in a magic bakery by a kindly baker who used a series of different shaped tins to prepare everything—carrots and chicken and potatoes—from the same delightful substance.

Maybe it was the fact that everything tasted the same that made it so comforting to me. There were never any surprises, good or bad. It was always the same, and always would be the same. No matter how ugly the situation in the hospital, no matter the kinds of war going on within the human body, that magic baker would always come through, as he did that first morning.

I was never fancy about food on the outside. All I needed was something I could hold down. As long as I could do that, I'd be fine. It could be a bag of chips and some beer, or a steak and some beer, or a couple of slices of bread, or a handful of breakfast cereal. Hospital food was fundamental sustenance and nothing more. It was perfect that way. I'd just have to go without the beer, but I could do that. If I was going to have to survive and function without basic freedoms, I could do the same without beer.

When the breakfast cart was buzzed in through the double doors, even the people who seemed normal while sitting at a table slouched and shambled when they stood to walk, zombies moving in for a very slow kill. Patients appeared out of nowhere, sliding their feet slowly, barely lifting their slippers off the ground, arms at their sides, their eyes set dead ahead, and gathered in a rough cluster that moved toward the waiting cart, intent on a single goal.

The cart was loaded with covered plastic trays. From each tray dangled a slip of paper on which a name was written in large, clear letters. The patients surrounded the cart and groped at the trays, each looking for his own. The orderly who had pushed the cart through the doors backed away warily, perhaps out of fear of being bitten. Despite my hunger, I hung around at the rear of the crowd; I didn't want to get in anyone's way myself.

There was, much to my astonishment, a tray with my name on it. As she had promised, the nurse I'd spoken with that morning had arranged for something. Not much—coffee, orange juice, a muffin—but it was enough, the little something in my stomach I needed to get me going again. I sat alone at a table and ate happily, peeling the foil from the top of the wide-mouthed juice container, chopping the frozen pat of butter across the split muffin.

When I was finished, I filled out the menu card as instructed and returned it to one of the nurses. She looked at the name.

"Mr. Knipfel?" she asked, as I was turning to leave.

"Yes?"

"Your doctor is here today—he stops by every Saturday to see patients. You've been scheduled to meet with him at ten-thirty."

That was something I wasn't expecting. "Oh well,

very good, then." I smiled. I'd meet with him, he'd see how stable I was, and I'd leave this afternoon. Only one night here and I was no worse for wear, even if I hadn't determined who the mirror-shared culprit was. Not even the most ingenious police force in the world scores on every case.

I looked at the clock above the nurses' station. It was ten. To save time later, I might as well go get packed now. It wouldn't take long.

7. *drei*

The dark-paneled room I woke up in kept changing—and changing dramatically. When I first opened my eyes, it was the ground floor of the Classics Building at the University of Chicago, with its tall, narrow smoke-stained windows, its stone staircase curling up to the right, and a small, battered wooden bench directly in front of me. Then it was a simple white corridor, like you'd find in a hospital, with rooms across the way. Once it was a Technicolor, Panavision open plain—blowing grass under blue sky, clouds—with an enormous grainy black-and-white locomotive bearing straight down on me. I squeezed my eyes shut and waited. I heard no train chugging relentlessly onward, I smelled no thick, hot diesel fumes. When I reopened my eyes it was gone, replaced with the original dark paneling.

Soon people started coming into the room—not only my family and students of mine, and the expected regular medical staff, but also public relations people, media types who were arranging a press conference and a banquet for me the next day.

An orderly wheeled me into another room, where, I was told, the banquet was to be held, and even with the commotion of people putting things together, it looked mighty elegant. White tablecloths, floral centerpieces, china, silverware, crystal wineglasses. On one long table was an array of microphones. The orderly wheeled me around, let me take a good look at everything, then wheeled me back to my room and left me alone.

While I lay there trying to interest myself in what I could see in the hallway, trying to keep track of whatever hallway presented itself to me, a skinhead in complete Brownshirt regalia walked by: shiny black jackboots, armband, cap. He cast me a glance and kept walking. Something went cold in my gut.

A few minutes later, another Nazi walked by, headed in the same direction.

As the afternoon wore on, I watched more of them pass by and gather. They would stop and whisper at the bottom of the stone staircase of the Classics Building, laugh, then disperse in different directions. As a group of them went by my doorway, I recognized a kid near the back as one of my better students at the time. Skinny, bright kid. I couldn't think of his name.

"I hate you," he mouthed silently at me as he walked past, hurrying to catch up with the group. There was a cool, dead evil in his eyes I had not seen before. He'd seemed like such a nice kid in class.

When the Nazis gathered at the base of the stairs, I occasionally caught a hint of their whispers. A word or two would float my way, and although I didn't catch many, those few were easy enough to put together.

"Bomb."

"Banquet."

"Tomorrow."

They were going to blow up my big banquet? Why? I'd done nothing—at least as far as I could tell—to offend them. Maybe it was all the media attention. I strained to hear more details, some justification maybe, but nothing came through.

Nobody else seemed to notice them.

A nurse came into the room with a package for me—a gaily wrapped bright-red box with a huge black bow. I tried to tell her about the Nazis, but nothing came out of my throat. I still couldn't speak, and I had nothing to write with. She offered to open the package for me. I nodded.

She untied the bow, set the ribbon on the table next to the bed, carefully pulled the tape from the wrapping paper, removed the paper, folded it neatly, and placed it on top of the ribbon. She set the box on the edge of the bed and lifted the lid.

Three huge black Norway rats scurried out of the box and slid to the floor, clutching at the sheet as they scrambled down. The nurse didn't appear to see them. If she did, she didn't react at all.

She reached deep into the box and pulled out a gnawed and wiry mess of stems that might once have been a flower arrangement. She held it before my eyes so I could see it.

"How beautiful!" she crooned. "But whoever sent it didn't include any card." She peered into the box to make sure. "You must have a secret admirer! Well, I'll just leave it right here so you can see it."

She set the bowl of dead and broken brown stems on a table to my right. I winced. I wanted to tell her to remove it. I needed a way to communicate with her, but she was gone. Besides, at the moment I was more concerned about where the three rats had gone. They hadn't left the room yet. Not as far as I could tell. They were enormous, and probably hungry. The flower arrangement wasn't that big.

Was it just a warning, or had the Nazis decided to kill me with these rats instead of the bomb? It was like something out of Hitchcock—except that I couldn't see coming through it alive in the end.

Sometime later, another nurse entered the room with a covered lunch tray. She set it on the bed table in front of me, untied my arm straps, and disappeared.

I stared at the brown plastic cover on the tray. I hadn't recognized the nurse. She might very well be one of them.

As I stared at the lunch tray, I thought of *Whatever Happened to Baby Jane?*

I pushed the tray aside, lay back down, and felt a tug on the sheet to my right. I leaned over the side of the bed to look.

One of the rats, red eyes luminous, tiny yellow teeth reflecting the fluorescent light, was crawling up the side of the bed. I closed my eyes tight, then opened them. That had gotten rid of the train easily enough. But the rat was still there, only closer, its eyes fixed on mine. How do animals know to look into your eyes?

Thank God that nurse had untied my arms.

I flung the lid from my lunch tray to see nothing but lunch—chicken of some kind. I grabbed the cellophane packet with the plastic knife, spoon, and fork inside, poked the knife through one end of the cellophane, and turned toward the rat. I jabbed the knife at its face. It paused, moved its head to deflect the blows, yet kept crawling, dragging itself slowly up the sheet toward me.

I slashed at its paws, but the plastic knife was a hopeless defense. Instead of stabbing the rat, I tore a hole in the sheet a few inches in front of the little bastard—a hole big enough for it to fit through. And when it reached the hole, it crawled in and disappeared. As long as I couldn't see it, I figured, it wasn't a threat.

I wasn't in any mood for lunch anymore. I just needed to get out of there.

As though someone at the front desk had been reading my thoughts, two orderlies appeared. They unhooked
a few latches and wheeled my bed into the hallway. They
continued to wheel me down corridors, through an emergency room, and through a set of double doors into the
back of a waiting ambulance. They shut the doors, then
walked around to the front, climbed in, started the engine, and pulled away.

Feeling free at last from the menace, I slept.

At ten-thirty sharp, I was back in the day room, waiting. It wasn't long before a man wearing a crisp suit underneath his open white hospital coat approached the front desk. He looked like a shrink. He was tall with gray hair, wire-rimmed glasses, a beaked nose, and a tan on the fringe of a Minneapolis winter.

The nurse pointed toward me. The man looked, then turned to say something to the nurse. They laughed; then he crossed the floor. His stride was brisk and confident. In my eyes, he was too sure of himself. I didn't know whether to be relieved or concerned that it wasn't the doctor from earlier in the morning. He had struck me as an ultimately reasonable fellow. He hadn't spoken to me as if I were a lunatic or a child.

"Mr. Knipfel?" this new doctor said, sticking his hand out, unsmiling. "I'm Dr. Spellman. Could I talk to you for a bit?" His voice was well modulated and professional. It sounded as if he worked hard on it, practicing for hours at home every night.

"You sure can," I said, maybe too enthusiastically. I needed this man's signature. I wanted to get this over with, and I wanted to get out. "Where? Out here?"

"No, no. There's a room in the back that we use. We'll go there."

I took my book and stood up to follow him. We walked toward the hall full of doorways and I saw him gesture to an orderly at the nurses' station, a heavyset blond kid who appeared to be about my age. Early twenties. All the orderlies were blond. I hoped it wasn't the result of some twisted eugenics experimentation being conducted in the caverns beneath the hospital, but instead just a Minnesota thing. When we reached the last door on the right in the hall, Dr. Spellman stopped and pulled out a set of keys. He unlocked the door to let us in.

The room was huge, well appointed, and lush. Soft couches and easy chairs; an enormous polished desk; a large round oak table in the middle. Small lamps on end tables and the desk cast a warm glow. The windows were rectangular and the walls here met at right angles.

He moved to a chair at the central table and gestured for me to take a seat. I accepted. Despite how the rest of the room appeared, the chair was straight-backed and uncomfortable. I leaned forward and put my elbows on the table. The orderly entered the room quietly, closed the door, and took a seat in a comfy chair in a corner.

Dr. Spellman sat across from me and flipped through my file, which had been waiting on the table in front of him. Everybody had a copy of my file. Having learned the day before about the "psychotic break," I was more curious about what was in there—and what all the ward employees might know about me that I didn't know myself.

I turned toward the orderly.

"Why are you here? To make sure I don't go nuts and try to kill him?" I laughed, alone.

"Jason's here in case I should need him for any reason," the doctor said, with no further explanation.

"Uh-huh." An awful lot of geniuses throughout human history had been certifiable, but I was living proof that it was just as easy for an idiot to lose his mind.

"Now," the doctor said, looking at me over the top of his glasses, "it says here your roommate had some trouble last night."

"I told the doctor this morning—Dr. Ford?—that I didn't see anything. The orderlies woke me up."

"And he didn't offer you anything?"

"No sir. I slept right through whatever he did. And believe me—I'm keeping my ears open. If I knew anything, I'd let someone know." *Sound helpful,* I chanted silently. *Play the lackey. He's the man with the keys.*

"Good. We hope so." He flipped through more pages in my file. I tried to read them, but it was impossible. They moved too fast, the print was too small, and they were upside down. "How are you feeling today?"

"Great," I said. "Got some rest—I mean, apart from

the ugliness last night—got a shave, got something to eat. I'm doing just fine." I smiled broadly at him.

"Mm-hmm. Yes. You know, that's what worries me." He set my file down. I felt a twitch in my stomach.

"Pardon?"

"You seem to be doing almost *too* well."

"Pardon?" I repeated.

"James, look at this. Not too long ago, let's be blunt here, you tried to kill yourself. Now you're smiling and you say you're doing great. That concerns me. That makes me a little suspicious, I have to admit."

That makes two of us.

"Well, okay." I started talking too quickly, trying to cover myself. "I can understand what you're saying, why you might be suspicious, but let me try to explain the way these things work with me." I paused and took a breath, tried to slow myself down. "This is not my first attempt. I'm sure that's in your file, there. And these attempts are very cathartic for me—after I try, I feel cleaned out, happy. Relaxed. It empties all the bad thoughts right out of me. So, like I said, I'm being honest when I tell you that I'm doing very well right now."

"Uh-huh," the doctor said, as if I had just told him that my ideas could become wiggle-worms. Just like that social-worker woman had done.

We were silent, and I tried to reconstruct a smile, not knowing how to respond to his "Uh-huh." I'd have to wait for his next move.

He sighed. "Yes, that worries me," he said. "And that's why I think it would be best if we kept you here a little while. Just to keep an eye on you."

"What, until I'm miserable again?"

"No," Spellman said, "we'd like to keep you here to try to make sure that you never feel like doing this sort of thing to yourself again."

That sounded much more ominous than he probably intended it to. My stomach clenched up.

"How long are you t-t-talking about, here? Days? Months?" I had to stop myself from stuttering. If I stuttered now, everything would be lost. This whole scene was no good. Neither was my performance—first nearly gleeful, now panicking, all in the space of three lousy minutes.

"We'll have to see," he said calmly, though he seemed to glance toward Jason, ready to spring on my back at the good doctor's sign. "We'll play it by ear. I'll be meeting with you regularly, and we'll gauge your progress as we go along."

"How often is 'regularly'?"

He took a deep breath, pretending to read my file. "Oh, ummm, maybe once a week or so, to begin with . . ."

I'm going to see you once a week? I'm stuck here for weeks until you decide I'm well enough? I saw their plan clearly now—leave me in that torturous little room with all the weird angles, pop in once a week, and then, when I finally go completely insane, never having won that damned Pulitzer, decide that I have to stay forever. That didn't sound very good at all.

"I'm afraid our time is up," Spellman said, checking his watch.

I looked at my own watch—it had been ten minutes. Ten fucking minutes. I was going to get ten fucking minutes with this man once a week while I rotted in here? This is how they were going to make me get better? I could see now that I was just another pawn in another crooked game.

I'm not crazy! The Suicidal Tendencies song "Institutionalized" exploded in my head. *You're the one who's crazy!*

"But it was only ten minutes—" I stammered. The doctor raised a hand, cutting me off.

"Our time is up," he said with no uncertainty. "I have several patients to see today. Jason will let you out."

I sat there waiting for the prank to make itself evident, waiting for the idiot to smile, laugh, and tell me it was all a merry joke before signing my release papers. I sat and waited, until I felt Jason's heavy paw drop on my shoulder. Spellman wasn't smiling, and neither was Jason. I stood and let him walk me to the door.

"And James," Spellman's voice called out, "remember, if you hear anything about those mirror pieces, please let us know."

I didn't answer. I stepped into the hallway. Jason closed the door, locking me out. The corridor back to my room, back to the day room and my fellow inmates, grew to three miles long. I was going to be here the rest of my godforsaken life.

Dropping out a few weeks earlier had landed me not in a low-budget horror film, but in a dark absurdist comedy. Spellman was wrong, I knew that much. He just wasn't quite yet ready to admit it fully. And until he did, I was stuck.

This wasn't like stealing an armload of books and getting away scot-free. This new adventure was turning out to be a bit more extreme than I was used to—and a hell of a lot more than I was hoping for.

I came to the door of my room, started reaching for the knob, but stopped myself. I decided to stay out of my room as much as possible from now on, convinced that its very design was part of their insidious plot to knock me over the edge for good. I continued to the day room, toward a safer zone.

Even before I turned the corner, I could tell that something was terribly wrong.

What had been a place of relative silence and calm— a room full of crazy people that was quieter than any normal business office or library—had erupted into a cacophony of cracking voices and mayhem.

The two businessmen were on their feet, waving their arms at each other and screaming incoherently in a dispute over an empty paper cup. A two-hundred-fifty-pound woman with dirty-blond hair who before had been able only to stare at the floor was clapping her hands, stomping her feet, and howling in hysterical, frenzied glee over, apparently, nothing. The television room had exploded into mirthless hooting and hollering, which was leaking out from around the door and through the sealed window.

Nurses were scrambling for cover behind the counter of their station, two of them screaming into telephones, and orderlies—they *were* all blond—were hustling around, trying to calm the patients, who brushed them aside. The patients—most of them—were moving, on their feet, screeching or bellowing or chirping. It was as if the lithium, Thorazine, Stelazine, Trilafon, Navane, Haldol, and whatever the hell other psychotropics had been pumped into them had stopped working at exactly the same moment. One man crashed across the top of a table and rolled to the floor, then got up and did it again, hooting.

I glanced toward Edna, who was still unmoving, and who gave no indication that she noticed what was going on around her. I looked back to the large blond woman, who now was savagely banging her forehead against a wall as a much smaller orderly tried to pull her away.

Hundreds of playing cards and checkers had been scattered violently across the floor. Patients who were perfectly normal and sedate fifteen minutes earlier, when the doctor came for me, were trembling, curled up in fetal position, clawing wildly at their own flesh, weeping, laughing maniacally. Chairs were toppled backward and fists were being pounded on tabletops.

"Pretend to be perfectly normal and sedate until he gets the news," I imagined the nurses whispering to each of the patients who approached the counter for pills or cigarettes. "Once he finds out, you can return to your regular routine, okay? It'll be funny."

For the first time, the ward looked like all the books I'd read and the movies I'd seen told me it would.

I stepped gingerly around the edges of the room and took a seat as far away from the carnage as I could get. I was in a corner near where the gaunt man was still racing for his life.

At least he's still quiet, I thought, as I watched the room disintegrating before me.

"RATHER BE IN A GODDAMN PRISON THAN IN THIS PLACE!" he bellowed, as if on cue, jolting me nearly out of my chair. "NO PLACE TO GO! NOTHIN' TO DO! GODDAMN MICKEY MOUSE! RATHER BE GODDAMN *DEAD* THAN IN THIS PLACE! NOBODY CARES ABOUT YOU, NOBODY TALKS TO YOU! GODDAMN DONALD DUCK!"

Still pedaling, he inhaled deeply to prepare himself for the next volley of invective.

"SIT HERE WITH MY MOUTH FULL, SIT HERE

WITH THESE PRICES! DOCTORS, DENTISTS! ALL
THE TIME THEY CHECK ON US, OUR BACKS ARE
TURNED! OUR BACKS ARE TURNED! LIKE MIN-
NESOTA! LAST NIGHT I HAD CHEESE! GONNA
WATCH THAT FOOTBALL GAME—ON AT NOON!
SLOW DEATH! SLOW DEATH! UP TO FORTY!
DOWN TO THIRTY GRADUALLY!"

Then, as abruptly as he had started, he fell silent. He
continued pedaling, focusing now on the pointless
speedometer mounted on the handlebars. None of the
other patients paid him any mind, too wrapped up as most
of them were with their own active imaginations.

Once he stopped screaming, much of my panic about
my own circumstances dissolved, floating away into the
ether. I remembered that moment of delicious clarity
when I'd first come to in the hospital upstairs. There had
been an instantaneous flash when I knew that I was
insane—or in my case, that I had been insane. I remembered how happy it had made me to realize that the end
of all responsibility in this world was at hand, that there
was a whole new, unconnected world to discover.

As things around me slowly quieted down, as people
returned to their seats and orderlies picked up the playing
cards and checkers off the floor, I was delighted to know
that I was going to be here awhile. Knowing for myself,
deep in my heart—regardless of what that doctor might
have thought—that I was perfectly sane, I'd be able to

take in everything around me like an anthropologist. Every day would be a variety show. I looked around the room at my new friends, now thinking of them actually as my "friends," and felt content.

Yes sir, strangely, this is going to be okay.

On the couch by the double doors, Edna Malaise was crying, black streams of mascara running down her neck.

9 . Wrestling

It didn't take me long to fall into a regular daily pattern. Up at seven. Shower, dress, and make the bed. Move out to the day room about seven-thirty, read until nine, when the breakfast cart showed up. Eat, decide what I wanted for lunch, fill out the card and turn it in. Read some more, maybe even talk to someone until lunch showed up at twelve-thirty. Then do the same until dinner. Then do the same, and move back to my room about nine to go to bed.

That self-enforced Germanic structure made the first days pass as painlessly as possible. It was comforting, even relaxing, if a little dull. Before I ended up here, when I was still living in the modern world, every day had been filled with potentially disastrous mischief—drinking, stealing, fighting, grading papers. More than a few times it wasn't clear whether I'd get back to my apartment alive at the end of the day. And while there was certainly a romantic appeal in choosing to live that way, it was nice to take a break from it, catch my breath a minute before stepping into it again. My task now was to enjoy my time and wait for Spellman to realize he was wrong about me.

Much of every day—much of everyone's day on the ward—was given over to waiting. Waiting for meds. Waiting for smokes. Waiting for breakfast, or lunch, or dinner. Waiting to see the doctor. Waiting to go to sleep. Waiting for the screaming to stop. We were a roomful of Estragons and Vladimirs.

I was well prepared for it all, having become fascinated, even obsessed, with the process of waiting when I was first studying philosophy—existentialism and phenomenology, mostly. As an undergraduate I'd done a lot of thinking about waiting. Usually while waiting. I'd sometimes intentionally arrive at appointments half an hour early just so I *could* wait.

Far from the tedious and frustrating ordeal it seemed for most, waiting had become for me an exercise. In the notebook I always carried with me back then, I'd chart the ebb and flow of anticipation—trying to guess when the person I was waiting for would arrive, or marking the exact moment when I realized the person wasn't going to show. Most of the time that's what happened.

The conclusion I eventually came to was that waiting, however frustrating it could be, was essentially an optimistic act. If you're waiting for something, you're harboring the hope and the belief that it is going to happen. If you don't believe that, you don't bother waiting; you just go home and make yourself a sandwich.

While waiting on the outside, I would compulsively

measure out my actions. If I was waiting in a bar, for instance, I'd allow myself one swallow of beer every five
minutes until whoever I was waiting for showed. Sometimes I would open my notebook and scribble page after
page of stream-of-consciousness drivel, attempting to
record every trivial occurrence around me—both internal and external—which I would later type up and proclaim "literature."

Here, if there was nothing else to keep me occupied,
I could make a game out of waiting. Well, a game of sorts.
I could focus my attention—as subtly as possible, so as not
to raise undue suspicion—on a single patient. Register
movements, sounds, words, gestures. It would be a nice,
quiet way of getting to know people, and it seemed safer
than going into the TV room.

I was sitting at a table, occasionally looking up from my
book to watch the slow and steady line for cigarettes and
meds; I would probably never have to stand in that line. I
had considered it a few times—walking over and waiting
with the rest, just as a change of pace, just for yuks, but always talked myself out of it. What the hell would I do
when I my turn came? I'd only look foolish, and earn another notation in my file: "Patient waited in line for no apparent reason."

I counted eight in the current procession. There was

Eddie, near the front. Eddie was greasy and unpleasant, a little creep with dark eyes that darted from one person to another around the room, trying to figure out who would be out to get him next. Behind him was Jack, whom I liked. He didn't bother anybody, and I was finding I could talk to him—until the Haldol kicked in.

The major problem I had in trying to have a simple conversation with other patients, about the weather or the food, or their lives, was that most of them wouldn't talk to me. They would stare at the ground, or the table, or their hands, and remain perfectly silent. At most, they'd make uncomfortable, quiet meeping noises. Others would deign to speak only to a particular fellow patient. Then there were a few like Eddie.

Eddie the Paranoid, as I called him, had come to me the previous afternoon, my fourth day on the ward, to strike up a conversation. At first I thought it was a friendly gesture on his part. Of the other patients, only Jack had said so much as hello to me. I hadn't spoken to anyone apart from the humorless doctors, nurses, and social workers. With some embarrassment, I had to admit that I was becoming a bit lonely.

The conversation with Eddie I had been looking forward to quickly spiraled out of control. Once his clipped delivery, spit out between quick drags on an unlit cigarette, sped past the admission that he was the one who shot John F. Kennedy, the continued influence to this very day of the Trilateral Commission, the fact that They were slipping poisons into our food, evidence that the nurses and orderlies were alien operatives, and how a transmitter had been implanted in his brain by the CIA, Eddie started talking about clothes.

The Trilateral Commission and aliens I could handle, even enjoy. I'd long been intrigued by conspiracy theories, the more outlandish the better. But I'd never known anyone who had the patience to tolerate hour-long monologues about clothing.

I wasn't even sure how Eddie had done it. He'd slid from poisons to aliens just fine. But a few moments after he'd left corrupt Venusian politics for radio transmitters, he moved on to slacks. I was following things pretty well until he hit the slacks. That's when he started losing me. Now he was talking much too excitedly about socks.

"Most people overlook socks," he machine-gunned nasally. "Most people don't *understand* socks, y'know? Cover your feet and that's all, they think, y'know? But the material means everything, see? The *material.* Now, look at mine—" He sucked frantically on the cold butt as he spoke, tapping imaginary ashes off the end every few minutes. It was a torture, a cruel attempt to weaken me.

"Look, Eddie," I said after he'd begun the lesson on socks, "I'm gonna read now, okay? We'll talk sometime later." I hoped there was a way to avoid him for the rest of my stay. Most everybody else seemed able to do it.

"I'm not *finished* yet," he said, annoyed by the interruption. He went on from socks to buttons to pockets, then back to the CIA, until the dinner cart showed up, nearly three hours after we'd begun our chat. I was numb, almost too exhausted to eat. Later I learned that Eddie was talking to me only because nobody else would let him sit anywhere nearby.

After that conversation he had stayed away, content to glare at me accusingly from across the room. He'd decided that I was another one of Them, someone else out to get him, which was all right by me. If he ever started in with me about buttons again, I *would've* been out to get him.

As Eddie stood in line at the nurses' station now, his eyes scanned the room. They paused on me, narrowing, with each sweep.

It had been an easy day so far.

Then I heard the hoots, and something slam hard against the plexiglass window of the television room. I looked over to see what was happening. Everyone in there was jumping on the chairs and couches, flailing arms, screaming with a mixture of glee and outrage.

On the television screen—which I glimpsed among the flying bodies—two men in garish tights were throwing each other around a ring. I looked over at the nurses' station. Not at all like the previous Saturday: nobody was paying attention to the melee in the TV room.

Jack received his pills at the counter, swallowed them,

got a cigarette, and returned to his regular table in the middle of the room. He was an older guy, heavy, with thinning white hair combed neatly straight back from a wide forehead. He looked like Lawrence Tierney. Sounded like him, too, his voice a deep, meaty rumble. To look at him, even talk to him, Jack would probably strike most people as perfectly normal. A rough character, a tough guy, but one who could flow through life like water. And I got the impression that he had, for a while. Then he hit the rocks.

Jack had been an electrical contractor, he'd told me, until he started hearing the voices. One day the electricity itself started whispering to him as it coursed through the wires, telling him how to do his job. He was a nice fellow, but the medication must have slowed him down a lot. Mostly he just smoked and waited for the next meal to roll around, like everyone else. He'd get out one day, sure, but he didn't seem to care much one way or another when or if that ever happened. He seemed pretty satisfied to be where he was now. He was glad not to be hearing voices anymore, that's for damn sure. Especially voices that told him what to do.

"Hey, Jack." I pulled up a chair next to him. He was keeping an eye on the TV room, too.

"Hey there, Jim."

"Hey, so—what's going on in there?" I nodded toward the mini-riot.

"Wrestling. Drives 'em crazy every time."

"Crazy like that?"

"Yeah."

"Jesus, huh?" It was best, especially after he'd taken his pills, to keep the conversation simple.

"Yeah, you said it." He never looked at anyone he was talking to. We both watched as a sofa cushion bounced against the TV room window, then fell back to the floor.

"Why do they let them watch if it does this to them?"

Jack thought for a long while. "Ohh, guess it don't hurt 'em at all. Lets off steam. Better than goin' after the nurses, huh?" He made a grunting sound that I think was supposed to be a chuckle.

"Yeah, I suppose," I said, a little doubtful.

"Besides," he went on, slowly working his latest cigarette, trying to make it last, "they always keep it in there, and they always pick up afterwards. Clean up, you know? Quiet for a week after."

"Except for last Saturday, right? And nobody's been killed yet?"

"Naaahh . . . They got too much in 'em to hurt each other too much." I presumed he meant medication. He was silent again for a moment. "I still wouldn't go in there if I was you."

"Oh, don't worry about that." I was quickly finding that Jack was a good person to talk to. He'd been on the ward for several weeks now, compared with my five days, and could cut through the bullshit of what went on.

"Well, then, thanks," I said, standing up, not wanting to bother him too much. "I was just curious."

"Yeah, fine."

I took my own regular seat, moving the chair around so I could get a clear view through the window of the TV room. It was impossible to tell exactly how many people were in there, given the dim light and the commotion, but I could count at least six.

From the glimpses of the screen I was able to snatch among the flopping limbs, the patients in the room weren't just jumping up and down, cheering their favorite wrestlers and damning the villains—they were acting out everything they saw on the television, move for move. More slowly of course, as a result of the drugs, I presumed. I saw imitations of every headlock, and bumbling approximations of every body slam.

So that's why the walls are carpeted.

When the wrestling show ended, the TV room was quiet again. The only motion now, as Jack had predicted, came from the patients picking up sofa cushions and moving chairs back into place.

I couldn't wait to see what would happen when *Ice Capades* or *Wild Kingdom* came on.

My parents had driven up to Minneapolis from Green Bay as soon as the hospital called them about my overdose.

They moved in with my dad's sister, Dorthea, to stay close by until I was released. When they visited, I kept telling them it wouldn't be very long, just a couple of days tops. Every few days since I'd been admitted to the ICU, they stopped by to check in on me—which was more helpful than what the hospital itself was offering now by way of "treatment."

Not that I was looking for any treatment. My parents let me know that there was someone, still, who gave a damn about me, no matter what I'd done this time. They were reminding me that there was a world outside these walls.

When they visited the psych ward, though, my mom couldn't bring herself to walk through the double doors. She had done it once, and was confronted with the sight of Edna Malaise sitting on the couch, staring her crazy stare, sporting her zany tribal warpaint. After that, my mother waited outside, in a room down the hall from the ward. My dad would come to get me, and then we would join her, an orderly trailing behind to make sure I didn't make a break for it.

On their third visit while I was in the ward, my mother's eyes were still red-rimmed from crying; she'd been crying since they got the news that I was in the hospital. Her normally happy face was sallow from heartbreak.

"Those people in there," she began, "I just don't like

to think of you as one of them." The idea of having an insane son was bad enough, but I think she was talking about Edna specifically. Edna could put the big fear into anybody. Maybe that's why she sat just inside the doors.

"Oh hell, Mom," I tried to comfort her. "I'm not. They're being stupid about letting me go, is all. You know I don't belong here." I'm not sure she believed me. I'd been there only a week, but at night, before I fell asleep, the question of where I did or did not belong was beginning to whisper to me, too.

"That woman in there with the makeup . . . what's wrong with her?"

"Oh, Lord knows. She just went a little funny in the head somewhere along the line. Then she stayed that way, I guess."

My parents both grew up on farms in northern Wisconsin and until now had led lives untouched by anything resembling mental illness. They didn't know how to deal with it, or even what they were dealing with. I was the first person in the family to have a screw loose—at least in such a way that required institutionalization. It wasn't a status I was especially proud of.

We had a few crazies in the family—a couple of alcoholics, a few black-sheep uncles here and there, at least one obvious case of Alzheimer's, a few wild cousins whose lives were far from perfect. But as far as I was aware, no suicide cases. Certainly no one who had had to be locked up for going mental. That distinction was mine alone, and I felt pretty shitty about it—not so much for myself, but for putting my parents through this.

After one of their visits, as my dad was walking me back to the double doors, he told me quietly and seriously: "Please don't do anything like this again." He was remembering when I had cut my wrists and tried to hide it from them. "It's killing your mother. She simply won't make it if you do it again."

We stopped a few yards short of the orderly, who was waiting to have me buzzed inside. This was none of his business. I took my dad's hand and pulled him closer so I could whisper back to him.

"I'll do my damnedest," I said. What that amounted to, I couldn't say.

10. Tri-Zeta

Over the course of the first few weeks, I came to know most of the names and faces on the ward—even if I had to make a few of the names up. Turnover was slow. That was good. I had never been too quick with names and faces.

I had already met or identified Edna, Jack, and Eddie the Paranoid. The two distinguished gentlemen, I found out, were Darin and Peter, though I never determined which was which—and it didn't much matter, because they were always together, and never spoke with anyone else.

Everybody called the fellow on the bike Gus, and that seemed to fit. Nobody knew much about him, or how he'd ended up there, specifically; he had been a patient for as long as anybody could remember, and had always been riding that bike. (Maybe he'd been a compulsive bike thief; or maybe he'd once kept running people over on his bike; or maybe he was a bike messenger who just couldn't take it anymore. Speculation never got much further than that.) The big blond woman's name was Mary. Like me, she was an attempted-suicide case. She'd tried to gas herself, but it hadn't taken. While it didn't kill her, something had snapped in the process, leaving her damn near autistic.

Since I didn't have the access to files that the doctors and nurses had, and so didn't have the scoop on why a lot of these people were here, I had to count on what I heard from other patients—hardly the most reliable of sources. But while I might not know precise causes or diagnoses, the symptoms, even in the seemingly calmest of patients, were fairly evident.

Most of the people I watched move around me every day appeared as sane and normal as I was. They used plastic knives and forks with ease. They drank from cups without spilling much. Most of them bathed. Head-bangers were rare, but I caught sight of some. There were a few obsessive-compulsives—people who would combine the trash from their meals into the smallest possible pile (usually by stuffing everything into a paper cup), or who always walked backward around corners, or who rapped their knuckles on every table they passed.

Much of the time, if someone outside had peeked in one of the picture windows, the ward might have seemed less a madhouse than a small-town coffee shop. It was full of regulars who hung out all day, eating, smoking, chatting among themselves, playing cards, knowing everyone else's business to a degree. The only difference was that here, half of them stayed in their bathrobes all day, and every once in a while, somebody would start shrieking like a banshee.

I was sitting in my chair one Friday afternoon when I took a look around and saw the scene I'd viewed so many times before. Darin and Peter were talking amiably. Jack was smoking quietly. The line at the nurses' station was calm and orderly. Except for the slippers, I suppose, most of these people could've fit in most anywhere.

If I were to put that first Saturday's brief mayhem out of my head, and discount Gus and Eddie and the wrestling boys, the question was reasonable: What in the fuck were we doing in here?

Were we hiding? Were we deceiving ourselves? Were we being held hostage by forces we could never know? Or were we really insane, as we'd been told?

Hell, I knew people on the outside who were worse off than this lot. I'd been to wrestling matches and pro football games and seen more questionable behavior than I'd seen in the TV room that day.

A case in point was a guy I knew at the University of Chicago. His name was Harold Smudgen, and I've never known another human being who fit his name as well as Harold did. He was a full head shorter than I was, wore crooked glasses, always had a bad haircut, and was about as well muscled as the Pillsbury Doughboy. Harold was studying astronomy, and though he was full of radical ideas and grand notions about the structure of the cosmos, none of them was particularly imaginative or had any basis in reality. His professors would listen to him patiently as he outlined one new theory or another, then send him away with a kind smile and a pat on the shoulder.

Harold was a good guy, though—he was funny, if peculiar. He was also a slovenly glutton—eating near him was always a terrifying ordeal. Neither of us had many friends at Chicago; few people would talk to us, so we ended up talking to each other. We used to stay up until all hours, using Gödel's Incompleteness Theorem to disprove the existence of God.

What was remarkable about Harold, however, was that he was King of the Pigeons.

If it was a nice day out, Harold would usually have forty, fifty pigeons trailing behind him. He never fed them bread crumbs or popcorn, nothing obvious like that. No, Harold just . . . *cooed*. I'd seen him do it out of the blue. We'd be standing on a corner on the South Side, no sign of life around, and Harold would start cooing. Within seconds, pigeons would appear out of nowhere—out of the sky, out of the sewers, wherever pigeons come from—and cluster around us.

"That's really something, Harold," I'd tell him as I stepped carefully around the gathering flock of shitbats (as I knew them), withholding my urge to scream.

This story isn't really about Harold. To be honest,

being King of the Pigeons was his only claim to anything. No, this story is about Harold's mom, Mrs. Smudgen.

Harold came from a trailer park in a poor midwestern suburb. His dad and one of his brothers had a country-western band that played in the back of a pickup truck on weekends. His other brother, as far as I'm aware, always wore army fatigues. The whole family—under the leadership of Mrs. Smudgen—worshipped Elvis even more than I did. Harold had even constructed a shrine to the King in the corner of his dorm room.

Mrs. Smudgen was a powerful, mystical matriarch. She was one of those *Weekly World News* types, a New Ager who didn't buy into the sweetness and light of healing crystals, herbal teas, Shirley MacLaine and past lives. She was deep into the ugly side: monsters, UFOs, astral projection, psycho-command power, the King, and demons—*lots* of demons. Her world was jam-packed with demons of every order and variety, every shape and diameter. She was, she made clear, under constant siege from Satan's minions, all of whom attempted to drive her and her family from the one true path.

Mrs. Smudgen once ordered a book advertised in the *Weekly World News* that promised to give her the power to explore the deepest secret corners of her own mind, where she would learn the Great Truths of the Universe, which would allow her, finally, to dispel all those wicked spirits. She studied the book faithfully and carefully once she received it, then started experimenting on herself. To no one's great surprise, the methods outlined in the book worked like a charm.

On her first trip to Inner Space, Mrs. Smudgen found herself in the corner of a small, crowded, doorless room. Around her, creatures with various physical deformities stumbled about in a firelit darkness. She soon recognized these creatures as her own children—one with hands but no fingers, another with shriveled legs. A voice boomed over the room's PA system:

"Welcome to your own corner of Hell!"

Upon returning to the reality of a trailer park, Mrs. Smudgen realized that each of the deformities had some significance: her guitar-playing son had had no fingers; Harold, who loved walking, had had shriveled legs. She took another trip to learn what it all meant.

She found herself in the same place, but now there was a door in the room. She knew that Great and Profound Knowledge awaited her on the other side of the door, but that if she went through it, she might never return to the world of the living. That, she seemed to know intuitively, was the price of acquiring this arcane wisdom. She came out of her trance without going through the door, and then burned the book, to prevent Harold from getting his hands on it.

"You would walk straight through that door without thinking, and never return," she told him. A week later, after much serious contemplation, she went back into a trance, back into the little room, and through the door.

Well, mercifully, Mrs. Smudgen eventually awoke from her trance. But this time when she came back, she spoke to nobody, made no dinner for the family that night. Instead she sat on the sofa with a spiral-bound notebook and started writing—something her family had never seen her do before.

After a few days, she stopped writing. Apparently, on the other side of that door, she had been given the knowledge of "Tri-Zeta," a complex collection of Nostradamus-style predictions for the future. It was these she had transcribed into her notebook, in rhymed couplets.

Now, I don't know any of the secrets of Tri-Zeta myself because, beg him as I might, Harold never photocopied her notebook for me. I can tell you this, though: Mrs. Smudgen had no prior knowledge of even minimal Greek. It wasn't until several months later that a friend of hers pointed out that zeta was the sixth letter of the Greek alphabet. So "Tri-Zeta," of course, meant "three sixes"— the Mark of the Beast.

The rhymed couplets contained the secret wisdom concerning the battle of Armageddon and the coming apocalypse. Mrs. Smudgen was frightened of what she had tapped into, and fearing that it all might be the Devil's handiwork, she burned the couplets, just as she had burned the book that gave her the power in the first place.

While all this was happening, I was getting as much mileage out of Tri-Zeta as I could. If I was taking a test and hadn't the foggiest notion what an answer might be, I simply wrote "Tri-Zeta," figuring it couldn't possibly be wrong. One day there was a huge student demonstration in front of the university's administration building. I had nothing to do with the demonstration and didn't know what people were so upset about, but I bluffed my way to a microphone and told the crowd, "People! Students! Listen to me! I'm going to walk into that fucking administration building and get the answer we're all waiting for!" The protesters—they're so dim sometimes—cheered as I turned and walked through the doors.

Actually, a friend of mine was working in the building at the time, and I had been on my way to say hi. I did that, came outside a few minutes later, took the microphone again, and announced, "People! I have just met with the pigs in charge! I demanded an answer! They *gave* me an answer! People, *listen to me!* The answer is ... *Tri-Zeta!*" Then I got the hell out of there.

Yes, that kept me amused for quite a while.

Back in Mrs. Smudgen's neighborhood, a film company was scouting location shots for a Gene Hackman feature. The company chose the Smudgen residence for some of the interiors. They moved out the old furniture and brought in new, painted the walls, remade the place real nice. The director was so taken with Mrs. Smudgen that he allowed her to stay around and watch the filming.

In between shooting, the director and Mr. Hackman sat on the new couch with Mrs. Smudgen, listening intently as she told them about the mysterious message of Tri-Zeta. When the filming was over, the crew had come to love Mrs. Smudgen so much (or maybe they were just scared of her) that they let her keep the new furniture. Mr. Hackman promised to visit whenever he was nearby, and has sent her a nice Christmas gift every year since then.

Point of all this being that had Mrs. Smudgen shared her theory or her couplets with a psychiatrist, she would have been in here with the rest of us. Most of us were no crazier than anyone else, I was beginning to think, except that we were stupid enough to share our quirks with a medical professional of some stripe. With a few obvious exceptions—Eddie the Paranoid struck me as someone who might be dangerous—the rest of us seemed just *fine*. Our only problem was that we'd made the mistake of going public.

One day during my second week in the ward, I was eating my breakfast alone, as I always did, at a table next to Darin and Peter's. For once I was able to overhear what they were talking about. I'd tried to eavesdrop before, but they spoke too quietly, and I'd never been close enough.

They were wearing their own bathrobes—not hospital-issue—and nice slippers on their feet as they ate matching breakfasts of scrambled eggs, toast, apple juice, and coffee. They were having what appeared at first to be a sophisticated discussion concerning the fiber and cholesterol levels in their food, the diets they were trying to stick to in this place, and the importance of good nutrition. There was nothing out of the ordinary, it was boring, even, not worth listening to, until one of them—I still couldn't tell them apart—slipped away from food science and the other followed.

"I like Cheerios," Darin or Peter announced.

"I like Swanson TV dinners," the other replied.

"I like sherbet. There are four flavors."

"I've had lime a few times."

"Well, raspberry's the best."

"A friend of my brother's works in a wheat field. I talked to him about Wheaties once. He said it's better for you if you just eat the box."

"I've done that."

"I like toast."

With that, having evidently communicated all they needed to on the matter, Darin and Peter fell silent. A moment later, without having spoken another word, they got up and left the table with their breakfast trays.

Ahhh. So that's why they're here.

Then another thought elbowed me lightly: If these two normal, sedate, distinguished-looking gentlemen were jackass crazy, what about the rest of the people here? And more important—*Jesus Christ*—what about me?

11. *vier*

I was awakened by the foot of the bed slamming against the back doors of the ambulance, almost bouncing me onto the floor. Fortunately, the doors didn't fly open.

We were driving up a steep incline. Through the back window I saw old, decrepit buildings, burned out and washed out, windows broken. From nearby I could hear the crashing of waves, though I could see no water. The road we were on continued upward at an impossible angle, and we stayed on it for a long time, traveling slowly. From the window it looked as if we were driving up a snowless ski jump.

Finally the ground leveled, and we stopped. My parents got out of the ambulance, walked to the back, and opened the double doors. They had replaced the two drivers and had a wheelchair waiting for me.

"C'mon, Jim. Get into this instead," my dad said. My mom was holding a blanket.

I crawled out of the bed and slid from the ambulance into the wheelchair. They strapped me in, and my mom threw the blanket over my legs. I felt like an old man, hunched over, looking down at the wasted brown seaside village around me. I had no idea why they had brought me here.

We were sitting on a bluff that rose two hundred yards and jutted out over an expanse of water. I didn't know what it was—none of Minnesota's lakes was this big. To either side of us lay a jagged, rocky shoreline. At the bottom of the incline was the city I had seen out the windows.

The buildings were primitive, like something from a distant past or a distant future. They were all the same light brown, and had no distinct corners, as though the sea had worn them down in a way it had not touched the rugged shoreline.

The buildings had a lot of windows, squarish but smoothed out like the edges of the buildings themselves. These buildings—there were dozens of them—appeared deserted, until I caught sight of some movement around one of them. At first it looked like two people. Then a third was with them.

One, a woman, wore a long, colonial-style dress. She was leading another person by the hand, and they were followed closely by the third up a stone staircase carved into the side of a building. The buildings themselves might've been carved out of stone.

As the three figures worked their way up the steps, my

eyes gained strange magnifying powers, bringing the people into sharp focus, like a telephoto lens.

The woman in the dress, I could now see, was Elaine, whom I had been dating when I moved to Madison after leaving Chicago. I hadn't seen her in three years. The two men with her seemed anxious.

They have no reason to be so goddamn excited.

At the top of the stone steps was a large wooden door, constructed from heavy planks. There was something medieval about it. Elaine shoved it open, stopped to give the first man a long, hard kiss as she rubbed against his leg, then dragged them both inside. The door slammed shut.

At the bottom of the same building, but on the other side, another door opened. Three skinheads in Nazi uniforms came out, laughing and joking and shoving each other around. They were clearly up to something as they walked to the next building and entered through a ground-level door. I recognized one of them as T, the monster skinhead from Madison who'd busted my head open onstage at a punk-rock show.

I began to notice how hot it was.

To my left, from among the jagged rocks along the shore, four giant poles began to rise. Flagpoles, almost, but made of wood, and much thinner and taller. They were in a row down the shoreline like the legs of the alien machines rising out of the pit in *War of the Worlds*. When the poles reached their full height of a hundred feet or more, two skinheads shimmied up each one.

They got to the top and raised some smaller poles, about fifteen feet long, and tied them perpendicularly near the top of each vertical pole, forming crosses. Once the cross-poles were in place, each team pulled a string, and down rolled a banner—like the ones at the Nuremberg rallies. Three banners were red, white, and black; the fourth was black and orange. The air was still and thick, so the banners rolled straight down, unfluttered by any breeze. Now each team of skinheads pulled something out of the bags they were carrying—and stuck a severed head atop each of the poles. Blood splashed down the length of each banner.

My parents were horrified.

They wheeled me down the ramp toward the city. I slept again.

12. Frogs Got It Better

"I'M WATCHING THEM! I'M WATCHING THEM AND THEY'RE WATCHING ME, LUCY! TIME FOR A DOUBLE-LOCKED BRIEFCASE! THEY'LL NEVER ONCE SEE IN MY HEAD!"

Gus was riding hard when I got out of my fourth meeting with Dr. Spellman. The meetings were always the same. They were always ten minutes long. Jason sat in the corner just in case I decided to express my discontent. I would tell Spellman something real and, to me at least, reasonably rational—about my dreams or my childhood fears or my previous suicide attempts. He never had much of anything to tell me, except that I would be there another week, until he could evaluate my progress again. He was monomaniacal that way.

Then he would ask me whether I had heard anything about the mirror shards, and I would tell him no. I wasn't exactly putting all my energies toward snooping around and apprehending the culprit. After making a few quiet inquiries that got me nowhere, I stopped. I was no rat,

and I wasn't sure I wanted to play ball with the administration that was keeping me here, even if it meant that I
might get out a little sooner. Besides, the longer I spent
here, the more comfortable I was becoming. At least some
of the time.

I shared nothing quite that blunt with the doctor, of
course. I told him only that I was getting along swell—
sleeping okay, enjoying the food and company, even coming to understand that Jacques Lacan character a bit, and
discovering that Lacan didn't know shit about mental illness. Maybe French crazy people are different from Amer-
ican crazy people. French crazies probably work at it a lot
harder, reveling in their fabulous nuttiness.

I found it strange that I never saw anyone else go in to
see Spellman. I couldn't have been his only patient—there
were twenty-five to thirty of us on the ward. Yet while
there were obviously quite a few other doctors who
prowled and visited the ward, I never saw anyone else go
into a meeting of any kind. Never saw anyone else led
down that endless hallway. Maybe I wasn't paying attention—or maybe the people around me were all lost causes,
beyond any help except what the drugs could provide.

After each of my meetings with Spellman, I'd go back
to the day room, and hear what Gus had to say. We seemed
to be working on the same schedule: every Saturday morning about ten forty-five, he'd lose it for a minute or so, just
as I was usually tempted to do. Maybe Gus was screaming

on my behalf. Or perhaps he spent his time waiting, as I did, except he was waiting all week for the chance to express himself, at ten forty-five sharp, and had to devise a way to cram all his thoughts and emotions into a one-minute block of speech. Sort of like what I had to do with Spellman.

"FROGS GOT IT BETTER THAN US!" he announced to the room. "RATS GOT IT BETTER THAN US! FROGS OUT MY ASS!"

I took a seat nearby and waited until he was done before I opened my book. I would have loved to see what Mr. Lacan would have done if confronted with someone like Gus.

We were approaching Christmas, and I was almost feeling that I was breaking through that impossible prose. I was lucky enough to have come into the ward, and into this book, with a reasonably firm working knowledge of the theories of other once radical psychologists—not only Freud and Jung, but Wilhelm Reich and R. D. Laing as well—none of whom was taken very seriously anymore.

Now, given that I had little else to exercise my brain with—there was no ward library to visit—I read and reread Lacan's essays. "The Mirror-Stage as Formative of the I as Revealed in Psychoanalytic Experience," "The Function and Field of Speech and Language in Psychoanalysis," his interpretations of Freud, his theories about the unconscious and psychosis. What had initially appeared an insurmountable stone wall of gibberish was slowly becoming more, well, climbable.

A Half-Assed Guide to Jacques Lacan

The way I was reading it, at least in the essays I was concentrating on, most of Mr. Lacan's theories centered on language. People—whom he refers to as "subjects"—are defined completely by the words they use—which he refers to as "signifiers." Language, in some form, is the only thing we can use to represent ourselves to others; and so any sort of communication between two people is always mediated by these signifiers.

The way Lacan put it, "The signifier represents the subject for another signifier." It took me a while to understand what he meant by that; I had to think of it in terms of a court case, a lawsuit, say. If I were suing Eddie the Paranoid for boring me, we would probably both hire lawyers. I'd explain the situation to my lawyer, who would talk to Eddie's lawyer, who would, in turn, explain things to Eddie. Then Eddie would talk to his lawyer, who would talk to mine, who would talk to me. That seems to be Lacan's model of human communication. Except instead of lawyers, we just have the words flowing back and forth—which is also why we so often end up misunderstanding and misunderstood.

Communication is like a never-ending game of telephone. Signifiers, Lacan says, not only define who we are but also separate us from everyone else at the same time.

That's the simple part.

Taking a cue from Freud, Lacan says that, psychologically, we're all made up of two parts—a conscious part ("the ego") and an unconscious part (logically enough, "the unconscious").

The unconscious is formed first, when we're infants. As we learn the basic rules for living, as we go through the various traumas necessary to know how to function in the world—to walk, talk, deal with others—we bury these lessons and traumatic scenes away. "Repress" them.

Grammar, for instance. As we learn the rules of grammar, we repress them in the unconscious, and they become an unspoken part of who we are and how we talk. If we had to think about all the rules of grammar we were about to use before saying anything, talking would be a slow, laborious, agonizing process. Even more so than usual, in my case. In fact, if asked to detail all the grammatical rules employed in constructing a sentence like this one, most people, I'd guess, wouldn't be able to do it. I sure as hell couldn't.

The ego is what eventually arises out of the unconscious. The ego is the result of trying to find the words to express what we have repressed.

Many things that get repressed are experiences we find too horrible to think about—witnessing a murder, or doing something that we're profoundly ashamed of.

Things that get repressed are what Mr. Lacan refers to as "the Real," the actual events and memories that are buried in the unconscious. What are Real are those things deep within us which we literally cannot talk about. We simply don't have the words to describe them, yet they define who we are at any given time.

The primary job of the ego is to make up lies to cover up what's in the unconscious—as in explaining away a suicide attempt by saying, "I was bored, is all."

Because deception is the ego's primary job, Lacan says, we are almost inevitably wrong when we make any conscious judgments about our appearance, our desires, and our motivations.

It is possible for what's been repressed in the unconscious to reveal itself, though. That's what psychoanalysis is all about. Because the unconscious has its basis in language, and is structured in language, it reveals itself through language—specifically things like slips of the tongue, dreams, neurotic or psychotic symptoms, and jokes, whose punch lines are a kind of intentional slip of the tongue.

It's the job of the psychoanalyst to encourage a patient to speak about the things that are Real—those repressed traumas we don't have words for—because as the patient attaches words to something, the clearer it becomes to him. Paradoxically, the more clearly symbolized we make something by speaking about it, the less "Real" it becomes, that is, the less it becomes an unconscious source of nutty symptoms.

In contrast to normal medical practice, Mr. Lacan argues, the diagnosis and treatment of what's behind a particular psychological problem can't merely be read from a patient's outward behavior. You can't take a problem—insistence on wearing clothes backward, or obsessive nosepicking—and look the diagnosis up in a book the way you might for a skin disease. Two patients who are locked up for exposing themselves in public are, most likely, exposing themselves for two very different reasons. That's why it's the job of the analyst to study language, and that way penetrate the patient's individual unconscious to find the true source of his behavior.

This is something psychotropic drugs cannot do. (I never read anything in Lacan about it, but it seems he would feel this way.) Medications, if you buy into this theory, would simply mask the symptoms, and do nothing about the source of the problem.

The process of analysis, Lacan says, is supposed to be one of frustration. The analyst isn't there to provide the patient with answers; all he's supposed to do is ask questions, forcing the patient to dig deeper into his own unconscious, to uncover the source of his own problems, and to find the words to speak it. Once the patient is able to talk about it, the problem will go away.

This is an extreme oversimplification, I admit, and only scratches the surface of everything Lacan was talking about. But it's about as far as I was getting at the time, trying to unravel things on my own.

I began to think about my own case in terms of what I was reading. Was Spellman just trying to frustrate me? Was that his crooked game?

I doubted it. He wasn't asking me any fundamental, probing questions; he asked me only how I was doing, and how the investigation was coming along. Then he'd send me out to the common room for another week.

As a result of reading Lacan, however, I started listening more closely to what Gus might be revealing about himself every time he opened his mouth.

Maybe he was less crazy than we gave him credit for; maybe he was just having some trouble expressing himself. Or maybe the things he was expressing were much closer to "the Real" than most of us were used to hearing. Frogs out his ass, after all. Maybe, as he pedaled away on that bike, he was trying to condense his thoughts into minute-long blocks of expressive, revelatory verbiage. It wasn't his fault the words were coming out all silly—we weren't taking the time to listen to him closely enough.

The more I did listen to him, the more I began to gather something that, if still not completely rational, was at least more understandable than before.

The first time I heard him speak, for instance, he'd made those references to Mickey Mouse and Donald Duck. It hadn't occurred to me until I heard him a second time that a few of the nurses behind the desk called the ward "the Mickey Mouse Club." Not very considerate on their part, but maybe Gus had heard this, too. He certainly didn't seem too happy to be here. Maybe that was his code. He seemed paranoid about being observed, and he had every right to be that way. He'd also made that comment about watching a football game. The folks who controlled the television watched wrestling, but never football.

This was nothing but idle speculation on my part. I didn't know a damn thing about Gus's background. I had no guess as to why frogs might be coming—or might have come—out of his ass. Maybe in his own convoluted way, Gus was detailing the things that had been taken from him in the ward. That made sense. It didn't explain how he'd ended up here in the first place, though.

Of course it was entirely possible that he was just nuts, that he'd always talked this way, and the fact that I was starting to force some sense into what he was saying meant that I was beginning to slip some myself. It still seemed to me that everything I told Spellman during our meetings made perfect, logical sense. But who knows?

It was worrying me a little: The more I thought Gus was making a smidgen of sense, and the more I was convinced that everything I told Spellman was as logical as algebra, the more I thought everything that came out of *Spellman's* mouth was gibberish. Brutal weekly repetitions were robbing his speech of all meaning.

The clearer the hopelessness of my situation with

Spellman, the clearer it was that I really was on my own here, almost to the point that I could be my own therapist. I guess I had Lacan with me—however ludicrous he could be at times—and thought I had some simple common sense. That was a start.

No. Not "therapist." That was the wrong word. I wasn't yet convinced that I needed a "therapist"—or needed to *be* a therapist. My second day on the ward, I thought I'd be an anthropologist, but that wasn't right, either.

I wasn't an anthropologist anymore. I was more like a spelunker, trying to retrace my way out of what had seemed a straight, clear tunnel when I entered, but which had become more convoluted the further I traveled.

Jesus H.— Understanding Gus. I'm so fucked.

One Sunday, as I was sitting at my regular table, I heard a noise. It was almost a scream, but it was cut off, strangled halfway, swallowed. I looked up and around to find a source. It didn't take long.

Mary, the two-hundred-fifty-pound blonde woman, the one gas couldn't kill, was trying to crawl over the counter at the nurses' station. The three nurses on duty had backed up against the wall and were staring at her. One of the nurses had tried to scream, but had caught herself. Her hand was still over her mouth.

Well, there's a young person with something on her mind.

Mary had reached over the counter and grabbed hold of something solid on the other side, and was heaving herself off the ground. She had hoisted her thick, flabby right knee onto the countertop, and was trying to bounce her left knee up there, too—all the while emitting quiet, dry grunts from deep in her throat. None of the other patients was doing more than watching, perhaps silently cheering her on. That's what I was doing.

Before she could get her left knee up and over, four thick-necked orderlies were upon her, pulling her back to earth, then laying her gently facedown on the floor. Then, all gentleness flushed out of them, they dropped to their knees, yanked her arms behind her, and snapped what appeared to be handcuffs around her wrists. Gus, on the bike, never broke his pace.

In a move that surprised me, the orderlies hoisted Mary, still facedown, off the ground and onto their shoulders. They marched her double-time across the room and through a doorway next to Gus's bike, a few feet from where I was sitting.

As they passed, I looked at Mary. She appeared to be unconscious. Her head hung limp on her shoulders, bouncing along in rhythm with the orderlies' footsteps. It wasn't clear whether she had fainted, or whether they had given her a shot when they'd slid her to the floor.

Although the door they ran through was open only briefly, I glimpsed a hospital bed in the room where they brought her. It wasn't like the regular beds we had in our rooms. It was a real hospital bed, high off the ground, with bars on the sides, the bars heavy with leather straps.

Behind the counter, the nurses laughed nervously and tried to calm one another. The patients, if they had even bothered to look up, went back to what they were doing, as if nothing had happened, or as if it happened often enough to be commonplace. I considered going to ask Jack what the hell that was all about, but before I had a chance, the door to the room reopened, and the orderlies— including Jason—streamed out and dispersed. Behind them, in the bed, I saw Mary strapped down tight. She was trussed up in what looked like an old-fashioned strait-jacket. I didn't think they used those anymore, except in magic tricks. The door closed before I could confirm what I saw.

Little League baseball was very big in Green Bay when I was young, but I never played. I would've been beaten to death by my bat-wielding teammates, or their parents. My dad coached, though, and my mom worked in the concession stand at the ballpark, so every weekend during the summer when I was eight or nine I was there, running around, playing in the bleachers, making paper airplanes, eating hot dogs, not paying the least attention to the games. It was something I always looked forward to.

From my vantage point under the stands one day, I noticed a crowd gathering at the edge of the gravel parking lot. The crowd grew, and grew louder, so I brushed the dirt off my shorts and walked over to see what the hubbub was.

It took some effort to squeeze through the adults and teenagers who had formed a rough circle around, well, whatever it was. Nobody was moving, and by this time, nobody was saying much, but I heard a child's voice sobbing.

When I reached the opening that the people had surrounded, I saw a kid about my age on the ground. More than just my age, he even looked a bit like me—crew cut, horn-rimmed glasses, dirty white T-shirt, short pants. He was the one who was crying.

And he was crying, I discovered, because one of his bare legs had slipped through the spokes of a bicycle. The bike was much too big for him; it looked as if he'd tried to ride it and fallen off, and his leg had gone through the spokes. I'd always heard cautionary tales about things like that, but had never actually seen it. I didn't even think it was possible, yet here it was, with results more terrifying than I had imagined.

The wire spokes of the front wheel had sliced deep into the flesh of the boy's skinny pale leg, and the blood was flowing thick—down into his sock, dripping into a black puddle in the sand. Nobody was doing anything for him; we all just stood there watching him suffer. *Why aren't any of these grown-ups helping him? Why aren't I?*

A moment later, an older kid, apparently this boy's brother, broke through the crowd, dropped to his knees beside the bike, and started pulling the spokes apart in an attempt to free his baby brother.

That scene—the trails of blood running down that white leg—haunted me for years afterward. The leather straps against Mary's skin did the same thing.

Here in the psych ward, it didn't look as if Mary

should be waiting too anxiously for someone to burst through the door to loosen those straps.

Jason pulled up a chair and sat next to me, as if nothing had just happened. "Hey, Jim."

"Hey," I said, with more than a touch of suspicion. He had never spoken to me before, and I had no reason to trust him. To me, he was nothing more than Spellman's enforcer.

"What's that you're reading?"

I closed the book and showed him the cover. "He's a wacky French psychoanalyst," I explained. It would have been pointless to go any further.

"You understand all that stuff?"

"I'm beginning to. Some of it, at least." I let my suspicion slide momentarily, but then caught myself. After what I'd just witnessed, I wasn't interested in discussing subtleties of contemporary postmodern psychoanalytic theory. "Say"—I gestured toward the closed door— "what's the story there?"

"Mary got upset about something." Jason grinned as if he had a secret. "She does that every once in a while."

"Uh-huh."

"It's okay, though—it gives us a chance to practice."

"Practice." I didn't like the sound of that.

"Emergencies. All this stuff we train for."

Were they getting themselves ready for the day when we would all rise against them, dozens of mirror shards raised in defiance?

"Look, Jim." Jason leaned in a little too close. "You're not an idiot. I can tell that." He nodded quickly at the rest of the room. "You're not one of them."

"Though I have to say I feel like it sometimes," I interrupted. "How long is she going to be in there?"

"We'll see what kind of shape she's in when she wakes up." He looked at the door.

"You put her out?"

"Had to. She goes wild, and she's *big*. We give her a shot to calm her down, otherwise we can't control her. She's pretty strong. . . . She'll be out for a couple hours. Then we'll see if she wants to behave."

I thought about that, looking around at my fellow patients, seeing how well they were behaving, wondering how many of them had been given the same treatment in the past.

"That all sounds pretty grim."

"You don't know the half of what goes on here." Jason wasn't smiling anymore, and his voice had dropped to a whisper.

"After seeing that, I'm not too surprised."

He leaned back in his molded plastic chair. "Know what I'll do for you? I mean, just because I think you're okay?"

"Put me in a straitjacket?"

He didn't laugh, only smirked a bit. "No, but I'll show you the closet where we keep them. I'll give you the whole grand tour—the stuff they don't want you to know about."

I set my book down on the table, losing my page. This was more intriguing than the dense theorizing of a long-winded psychoanalyst who'd probably never seen the inside of such a place as this, let alone where they kept the straitjackets. At the same time, though, I was wary of Jason's intentions. I'd seen what he and his pals could do to people who didn't behave. He was a kid, this Jason, whose eyes betrayed nothing, who spoke with the clean, smooth, pot-dulled tones of the jocks who used to torment me in junior high. His co-workers were big Minnesota boys who'd been put in charge of policing the mentally ill. Who knew what sort of cruel frat-boy shenanigans they might have planned for me?

"It's not a trick, is it? I mean, I'm not going to end up like Gus when it's all over, am I?" I indicated the exercise bike. Despite what I'd been thinking about him lately, "Gus" remained the ward euphemism for someone mad beyond hope of any kind.

Jason smiled. "You never know."

I went to my room, as usual, about nine. Instead of showering, brushing my teeth, and going to sleep, I stayed up

and waited. Jason said he would stop by my room sometime after ten, which was lights-out for the ward. Most
employees would have gone home by then; one nurse
would remain at the front desk, an on-call doctor who
rarely showed his face would be hiding somewhere in the
back, and Jason would be making the regular room checks
that night.

At ten-fifteen, my door opened a crack. Jason put a
finger to his lips, signaling me to be quiet. I rolled off the
bed and followed him out the door.

What in hell was I getting myself into? "Gee, Officer,
we have no idea what might have happened to Mr.
Knipfel. One night he just disappeared. . . ." I put that
thought out of my head, knowing I'd be kicking myself
later if I didn't take Jason up on his offer. Regardless of
what happened, and what foul chicanery I might be
falling prey to.

Jason, still dressed in his whites, gestured for me to
follow him. I tiptoed down the hallway in my stocking
feet, afraid my slippers would squeak too much on the
polished tiles and give us away.

The more I studied Jason, the more it seemed he was
just a kid. He was no older than I was, certainly, and possibly a few years younger. He looked behind us, to gauge
whether we were far enough away from the prying ears of
the nurse at the front desk. He walked a few more yards
until he was sure, then stopped.

"You wouldn't believe the stuff they still do here," he

whispered. "Look at this." He pulled a ring of keys out of his pocket, trying to keep them from jangling. He found the key he wanted, and inserted it into the lock on a gray door marked "Authorized Personnel Only." He turned the key and pulled the door open quietly. Inside were restraints of every variety, enough to amply stock your own S&M dungeon. A dozen straitjackets, hanging neatly side by side like ugly sport coats, the straps dangling to the floor. Handcuffs. Thick leather straps like those on my bed in the ICU—and those on Mary's bed, as far as I could tell.

"We don't use these very often," Jason said. "I mean, the drugs they hand out seem to keep these nuts here pretty well under control. But we need 'em every once in a while—like today—and the people in charge here have no problem with us tying people down if they think we need to."

The way he used "nuts" nagged at me. He wasn't part of the club. He wasn't one of us. I wasn't completely convinced that I was "one of us" yet, but I was a damned sight closer than Jason. Coming out of his mouth, the word betrayed his obvious contempt. But I let it pass. I'd said plenty of ugly and merciless things in my time. I was sure I'd be saying more of them, too.

He closed and locked the door again, then tested it before we continued. "This down here is amazing," he said, heading down the hall with a nervous glance over his shoulder. I kept an ear open to the patients' doors on the right, listening for any movement. I still wasn't sure why

Jason was doing this. All he knew about me he'd learned sitting in the corner during my pointless Saturday meetings with Spellman. That sure wasn't a hell of a lot.

Near the end of the hall, almost across from the room where I met with Spellman, he stopped in front of another door marked "Authorized Personnel Only," and pulled out the keys again.

He opened the door and flicked on the fluorescent lights.

It was a small, windowless room with white walls. A bank of silent electronic equipment stood against the wall to my left as I entered. In the center of the room was a long medical examination table, upholstered in black leather, with a little square leather pillow at one end. Three sets of wide leather straps were draped across the top of the table.

Jason closed the door behind us, and I began to sweat. *What's he going to do to me?*

"This is where they do all of their ECT stuff—electroconvulsive therapy."

"Shock treatment?"

"Yeah. It does wonders for depression."

"Man, oh man. They aren't planning on doing this to me, are they?" I asked. I couldn't take my eyes off the table.

"I dunno. I can't say. I doubt it. . . . They don't use it all that often. I never know until an hour or so beforehand. C'mere, let me show you this. . . ." He walked around the table to a door on the opposite wall, and I followed. I was sweating badly, and my stomach tightened, as an easy escape route moved farther from my reach.

He opened the door and flicked another light switch. It was another small, windowless room with white walls, and carpeting on the floor. This was more like the TV room, with a comfortable couch and a few upholstered armchairs. At the front were a television set and a VCR. An unlabeled black videocassette sat on top of the VCR.

"The day before they do it, they bring the patient and the family in here. They walk them right past the table and show them this tape of them actually doing it to someone. Can you believe that shit? They show the whole procedure, from start to finish. Explain everything, then let them decide whether or not they want to go through with it. Most of them do. I mean, they don't force anybody into it, but for most of them, they think it's the last option."

I wanted to ask if I could see the tape, but that didn't seem to be on the agenda. Not now at least. I was afraid that I'd be seeing it soon enough.

"Shoot all this electricity through someone's brain," Jason continued, almost as if he was talking to himself, amazed at the idea, "and they have like an epileptic seizure. What they do these days is, they give the patient all sorts of muscle relaxers beforehand—really pump 'em full—then knock 'em out, so they don't thrash around at all. They still have a seizure, but it just doesn't show."

"Ouch."

"Nah, that's just it—they're so out of it at the time, they don't feel or remember a thing. I've seen people sleep for three days afterwards."

"Gimme gimme shock treatment," I muttered. The psychiatric profession had come a long way—or maybe not that far at all—since the "Bath of Surprise." In the Middle Ages, the deranged were dropped unexpectedly through a trap door into a tub of ice water, in the hopes that it would shock the demons right out of their system.

I looked around the room. At first glance, it looked like somebody's rec room. It could've been lifted straight out of most any mid-American basement. Knowing where it was and what it was used for, though, gave it an aura of menace and cold horror. This wasn't a room for relaxing on a Saturday night. This was a room, as Jason himself had put it, of last options.

"It's still my job to help hold them down when they do it," he went on.

"Even with the straps?"

"Yeah." He moved to the door and shut off the lights. I was relieved to get away from that couch and that VCR. We went through the first room, and when he reached the door to the hallway, Jason opened it a crack and peeked out. It was clear. He turned off the lights and we stepped outside. He locked the door, tested it, and we tiptoed back toward my room.

"That's it?" I whispered, shrugging. "That's all the scary stuff?" I was disappointed. I felt let down.

We reached my door, and Jason gestured that he would follow me. Once inside, he asked, "What did you expect?"

"Cages, torture baths, something with spikes? Something really brutal."

"Don't need it anymore, I guess," he explained. "We've got the Time-Out Room, and we've got the ECT room. Drugs do the rest."

He was right, of course. When I looked around the day room, I didn't think any of these people were going to cause trouble. There seemed little need for external torment.

"What about the really violent cases, though? What do you do with those?"

"They don't come here," Jason said, shaking his head slightly. "They get sent someplace else."

"Oh." I found that vaguely disappointing as well. "You mean nobody ever slips through?"

He thought a moment. "If you want to count somebody handing out weapons to the nuts . . ."

Again with the mirror. Was that what this was all about? Trying to squeeze some information out of me? Despite my suspicions and ultimate disappointment, I thanked Jason sincerely, and shook his hand. I didn't want him to leave thinking that his tour, brief as it was, had been wasted on me.

"It's good to know these things are here," I whispered before he left to continue his rounds.

That night, for the first time since I'd arrived on the ward, my sleep was plagued by nightmares. Frenetic loud dreams involving electricity and Satan in a white doctor's coat.

I didn't see Jason again for three days. When I did, and waved him over to my table, he pretended he didn't know me. I was just another loon who was going to ask him how the economy was holding up on Orion that very minute, or accuse someone of stealing my bowling balls.

"Yeah?" he asked, looking stern and annoyed.

"Thanks again for the tour the other night," I said. "But I'm still not sure why you did it."

He looked around to make sure no one could hear us.

"I wanted someone from the outside to see," he said. Then he went back to the nurses' station.

I guess it was nice that he considered me someone from "the outside." Unfortunately, he didn't seem to notice that I *wasn't*. I was still in here, inside, and feeling more and more like I belonged.

Christmas came and passed without much noise or tussle. A small wreath appeared on the wall inside the nurses' station, but there were no candy canes, no visits from Santa, and no caroling or special musical programs of any kind. They might well have been offered upstairs, in the cancer ward and the burn unit, but they never made their way down to us. Perhaps the hospital administration and the visiting church groups felt it would've been a wasted effort.

My parents stopped by, naturally. They brought some new clothes for me, and some cookies, and a card. I felt bad that I had nothing for them. But what were my options? I guess I could've waited in line and gotten them each a cigarette, even though neither of them smoked. Or a couple of nice ashtrays. That was about the extent of my gift choices.

I did the best I could under the circumstances, and tried to act normal.

The day after Christmas, the wreath was gone. Nobody around me seemed to notice its absence any more than they did its appearance in the first place. I barely noticed myself.

14. Forgetting Names and Other, You Know, Things

Not many of my neighbors on the ward had visitors. A woman I presumed to be Mary's mother stopped by a few times. A small, weathered lady with long gray hair tied into a ponytail. They always vanished into the privacy of Mary's room for half an hour.

Most of the other patients didn't seem to mind not having visitors. Most of them didn't seem to mind about much of anything. The only exception was when the dinner cart was a few minutes late, or when they couldn't get a cigarette when they needed one. Visitors weren't an issue. They—or their absence—weren't anything to concern yourself with.

By the middle of January, my father was well recognized after having stopped by so regularly. Most of the patients seemed to know who he was, and the nurses knew him by name. I felt bad for the people who never had any visitors, who missed that shred of normalcy in what was otherwise, undeniably, a very peculiar form of day-to-day existence.

Visiting a locked-door psych ward isn't any fun for a normal person. I could understand how many of my neighbors on the ward wouldn't be much fun to be around, either. How do you chat pleasantly with a man in a bathrobe who is convinced that Eisenhower is out to rustle his cows?

I'd been pacing the day room for no other reason than to move a bit, to keep my muscles functional. I'd picked the habit up a few weeks earlier. It wasn't a symptom of insanity, though it probably looked that way to anyone who happened to be watching. I would cross the wide, bright room diagonally from the corner where Gus was pumping away and muttering quietly, to the opposite corner, where Edna sat on the couch near the double doors, then back again, zigzagging around scattered chairs and tables and other wandering patients. I was tempted to skip or jog now and then, to get a little more exercise out of the effort—hell, I was still a reasonably young man, and still had some energy left in me—but I didn't want to end up strapped down in the Time-Out Room, or worse.

Except for Gus's pedaling, and my own walking, I can't say as I ever saw anyone engaged in anything more strenuous than standing in line, or walking to the lunch cart, or opening the door to the TV room. Which might explain why everyone had a pasty, soft look about them.

It only made sense, if I thought back to Dante, and considered how many levels down we were. Thomas

Aquinas, I remembered, in his *Summa Theologica,* defined sloth—one of the Seven Deadlies—as a form of conscious, defiant despair in the face of God's goodwill. A form of heresy. Down here, despite Gus's best efforts and mine, we were, for the most part, under conditions of *enforced* sloth. Maybe the top brass wanted to ensure that those of us who were here for a while belonged here—and knew for ourselves why we belonged here.

Just more idle speculation, something to keep the brain working, the way I was trying to keep my legs working.

During one of my strolls past Edna, vigilant as ever guarding the front doors, I looked out one of the round windows, then stopped. Walking down the hallway to the ward was Bob Redden.

What?

Dr. Robert Redden was one of my professors—well, he *had* been one of my professors—at the university. He was a sociologist, and quite a big name in the field. I'd been a student in one of his seminars, "Theories of Social Disorder," when I'd taken the leap into the void the previous November. He was tall and slim, with a great globe of a head and a heavy, long black beard. He spoke in quick, nervous sentences that always had me wondering how, exactly, he had persuaded the natives of Papua New Guinea to trust him enough to let him in on the most secret secrets of their culture.

When he reached the doors, I was still standing there, staring. I gave him a wave. He picked up the phone and a nurse buzzed him in. When he opened the door, I saw that he was carrying a bright flower arrangement.

God, I hope those aren't for me.

He evidently didn't know about my overpowering and irrational fear of plants. Nobody did. Not even Spellman knew that plants—the simplest houseplant, the prettiest flower—terrified me to the core.

I had told Spellman about my fear of clowns, and my fear of getting ketchup on my hands, and my fear of being sprayed with garden hoses, among others. They might have seemed absurd, but the source of each of my fears was quite clear and justified in my head. But not my fear of plants. I wasn't sure where that one came from.

I could point to specific events for the others: the time the clown at the Shriners' circus ripped the balloon out of my hands to give to that monstrous little *blonde girl* sitting four seats behind me; the time the neighborhood kids held me down and covered my hands and face with ketchup when I was ten; the fact that whenever I passed anyone with a garden hose, I got sprayed with it.

As for the plants, the closest I could come to a source trauma was an episode of *Lost in Space* in which Will Robinson is being chased around on some desolate planet by a young alien hussy. When he trips and falls backward into a giant man-eating plant, it undulates and gnaws on him for a while. Scared the shit out of me, that scene. And now here was one of my professors, offering me some kind of plant—a collection of plants, no matter that they were cut, dead—that would undoubtedly attack and strangle me as I slept.

Unless he was hiding some rats in there.

"Hi," he said, nervously.

"Hey, Bob—welcome to my new home." I shook his hand, and he handed me the flower arrangement.

"These are for you. They're from everyone in the department. They all send their best." He was obviously uncomfortable here. I didn't know whether to attribute it to our surroundings, or to the fact that he always seemed uncomfortable about something. I took the vase from him, trying to swallow a scream.

"Thanks," I squeaked out. "C'mon in, I'll show you around."

"Thanks."

I turned and led him through the day room, pointing out various other patients. "That's Edna," I indicated as we passed. "Edna's job is to guard the gateway until her replacement arrives."

Redden nodded, confused. I didn't care. I went on with the tour.

"And that's Jack." Jack was sitting in his usual chair,

staring at his slippers, letting that hour's cigarette burn it-self out in the ashtray on the table. "Jack's job is to cut through the fog of reason. And over there in the corner, that's Gus riding the bike. Gus's job is to ride the bike." Redden nodded and made an almost interested twitchy sound in his throat.

"Do you have a . . . a job here?" he asked.

"Hard to say," I said. "I just wait, mostly. I think that might be it—my job is to wait. I've become a master of waiting for things." I knew it sounded cryptic, but what the hell? He was a sociologist. He'd probably heard worse.

"Oh," he said. It sounded as if he was set to turn and run already.

I led him around the corner, trying to hold the flower arrangement a safe distance from my body, so none of its poisonous tentacles could ensnare me. I opened the door to my room. "This here's where I stay these days," I told him. "Let me show you something remarkable about it."

He followed me inside. I set the vase on the bedstand and switched on the lamp. *Why didn't they check the plant? Why didn't Mrs. Whatsit follow us in here to make sure it was rat-free?*

"I'd offer you a chair, but I'm afraid I don't have one. You can sit on the other bed. I had a roommate when I got here, but he cut himself all to hell in the bathroom that first night, and they haven't bothered to replace him yet. I think they're afraid I have that kind of effect on people."

Dr. Redden made that twitchy sound in his throat again as he sat down across from me.

"So," he said after an uncomfortable lull, "how are you doing?"

I laughed. "You know, you'd be surprised. I'm actually doing really well."

"Everybody in the department sends their best," he repeated, perhaps out of having nothing else to say.

"Yeah, well, thank them for me, and tell them I'm doing great. With any luck, I should be out of here soon."

"Uh-huh."

"So am I missing anything?"

"Ohh." He looked around the misshapen room. "Nothing incredible. Nothing you won't be able to make up once you come back." He paused. "Should you decide you *want* to come back." I wasn't sure how to take that.

Maybe they thought that the university did this to me. Or maybe they didn't want me back, not really. Not after something like this. What if word got around?

"Oh, don't worry about that. I'll be back, all right. Why wouldn't I be? I mean, is there a reason?"

Dr. Redden shifted, only glancing at me. "Well, with everything that's happened . . ." His voice trailed off.

"And what's that, exactly? I mean, what were you told?" It was something I hadn't thought of. I had my folks call the department when I was still in the ICU, to let them know I might be in the hospital for a while. But I knew that my parents would never admit to strangers—probably not even to my sister in Green Bay—that I'd taken an intentional overdose.

"When your parents called, they said that you'd had a kidney failure, and that was all."

"Did you hear how I ended up in the psych ward?" I could also count on my folks not to lie. The kidney failure bit was true. If that's what they were telling people, fine then, I'd play along.

"No," he said, "we thought you were still in the hospital. I was just coming by to visit. It wasn't until I asked at the desk upstairs that I found out you were . . . well, down here. They gave me a pass." He showed me a slip of paper, which I ignored.

"It's an interesting story, actually," I told him. "In the first stages of the kidney failure, I had some kind of hallucination or something, like a really bad trip as a result of the renal backwash. It apparently went on for three days." As far as I knew, this might have been accurate.

Since I hadn't told anyone about the hallucination, nobody had been able to give me an explanation for it. It might've been toxins backing up in my brain—or I might've died and gone to Hell. I watched Redden's face for any sign of understanding, but saw none.

"When I got out of the ICU, I was told I was being sent down here for observation. They wanted to make sure that the hallucination hadn't been part of some large-scale psychotic break. That is, they want to be sure that I realize the hallucination was just a hallucination, you know what I mean? And that I'm no longer seeing crazy things."

"Uh-huh." I don't think he believed me one bit. Even people who know you treat you like you're out of your mind if, by luck of the draw, you find yourself in an institution.

"Only thing is, it's been an awful long time, and here I still sit. The doctor who can make the final judgment on my case is here only one day a week. So it's taken them a while to realize that I'm as sane as, well, *you.*" I waved in his direction.

"Uh-huh."

"But that's cool. I actually like it here. I like it here. Bed's comfortable, I like the food. And you never know what these people are going to say next."

I was hearing my voice for the first time in a long time. It sounded strange. The past several days, I hadn't been talking much, only listening. Sometimes that makes things easier. Talking felt odd now; it was an exercise in and of itself. Now that I had the chance to open my mouth, the words were coming out much too fast; they'd been stored up for too long. I was like Gus. Dr. Redden would probably go back to the department and tell them to write me off the books, that I was a lost cause.

"One thing that's making it tough, though," I went on, the words bumping into each other, "is this room. Look around this room."

He did.

"Notice anything?"

"It's a very nice room," he said in that frightened, patronizing tone I hated so much.

"No, no, no—it's *not.*" Something deep in the back of my head began screaming that I was about to blow it. But it was too late, I couldn't stop myself. I jumped up off the bed.

"Look at the way things are arranged—look at this room—the beds, the bedstand, the doors—you can't take a full step in any one direction. They designed this place to *drive* people crazy, see?" The words were spilling out faster and faster. *Oh, fuck it! You never liked this man to begin with, and besides, he brought you a plant that's going to kill you.*

"Look at those windows! You ever see windows like that? And the *walls*—there's not a single fucking right angle in this room!"

I was waving my arms now, pointing here, then there, and Bob was looking around, nodding, trying to follow where I was pointing.

"Yes, I see that now," he said quietly, almost to himself.

There was a knock on the door. It opened a few inches, and a nurse stuck her head in. "Jim? You have some more visitors."

"Oh, goodness—" I turned to Redden. "I'm sorry—I wasn't expecting anybody today. I wasn't even expecting you."

"No, that's okay," he said, standing up. "I should be on my way, anyway. I just wanted to stop by and see how you were doing and drop off the flowers."

"Oh, sit down, sit down." I waved my hands more. "Let's see who it is first." He sat down, but the expression on his face said that he really wanted to get the hell out of there and away from me.

Moments later, there was another knock on the door and it opened again. It wasn't my parents, as I had expected, but my aunts Dorthea and Janet, my father's sisters, and Janet's daughter Kelly, who was about seventeen.

"Well, lookit here!" I exclaimed, shuffling sideways between the beds toward the door, still overexcited. "C'mon in!"

Redden stood anxiously.

"Here, let me introduce you," I said, with another broad gesture. "Dr. Robert Redden, professor of sociology at the University of Minnesota, I'd like you to meet my aunt—" Then everything went blank.

I couldn't remember their names. Not for the life of me could I remember the names of people I'd known since I was a child.

"Ummm . . ." I began to panic. My hand hung in midair, frozen. *What are their names?* "My aunts . . . my aunts and my, ummm . . ." I couldn't even think of the word "cousin." My eyes went wide and darted from one person to another. "Oh Jesus, look at me. See?" I turned to Redden. "I told you this room was playing tricks on me."

Forgetting names, I remembered reading in Lacan, was no simple human error. It was a clear and definite sign of buried trauma. *Why can I remember that, but not their names?* I didn't want to think about it.

"Dorthea," my aunt Dorthea said, stepping forward and shaking his hand. "And this is Janet, and her daughter, Kelly."

"Nice to meet you," Redden replied. "Well, Jim," he said to me, "I know you all have things to talk about. I should be on my way."

Yeah, with a beautiful story to pass around the department, I bet.

"Are you sure? I mean—"

"No, I really should be going. My wife is expecting me." He had his chance, and wasn't about to let it go. He was getting out of here right now.

"Oh. Okay. Well, here, let me show you to the door—"

"Oh, I think I can find my way out."

"Let's hope I can too, huh?" I laughed weakly. "Thank you for the flowers," I lied.

"Sure thing. I hope to see you back in class soon," he said.

"Don't worry about it, I'll be there."

He worked his way through my relatives and out the door. I looked at my aunts and my cousin. "Sorry about that. I guess I just got a little flustered. I'm not used to having so much company in here all at once."

"That's okay," my aunt Janet said. The three of them sat down, Dorthea on my bed, Janet and Kelly on the other. I sat next to Dorthea.

"So," I said. "Here I am."

Dorthea and Janet worked in local hospitals, Dorthea as a head nurse, and Janet in a radiography department. Kelly, who was a junior in high school, had called me fairly regularly after I'd moved to Minneapolis. She was a good kid. Typical boyfriend problems and other teenage concerns, but she was cool. She had shown me around town the weekend I came to look for an apartment. It was good to see them now. Although I had plenty of relatives in the area, I'd been lax in contacting them since I moved here. I guess I was a bad kid.

"How are you doing?" Janet asked.

"Oh, I'm doing fine," I assured her. "I should be out of this place soon." I decided not to point out the maddening details of the room to them. It hadn't achieved the desired effect, I was finding. It only seemed to make people more uncomfortable. "It was nice of you to stop by."

"Are things going okay here?" Dorthea asked.

"Oh, yeah, yeah—they treat me fine. They just want to make sure that I'm okay before they let me go." I explained the official and highly suspect "psychotic break" theory to them.

Dorthea looked at me very seriously, very darkly. "You're a very lucky young man, you know," she said.

"Yeah, I know that, Aunt Dorthea."

"If you hadn't stumbled outside your apartment after your kidneys failed, do you know what would've happened? You would've died."

"I know that, Aunt Dorthea." I didn't tell her that had been the plan. I didn't see any need to get into it. Being where I was was bad enough. Apparently she'd been given the kidney story as well. No big deal. It was true. And it made things less creepy for everyone that way, I suppose.

The four of us sat on the beds for another half-hour, talking about how my folks were doing, about what other family members were up to these days. We talked about everything except my current situation. I didn't want to make the same mistakes with them that I'd made with Redden.

It might have been more comfortable, at least physically, in the day room, with more light and air and space, but I didn't dare subject any outsiders to that scene for too long. What if wrestling came on? What if Gus had some unscheduled idea he wanted to share with the rest of us? Mary's getting peeved about something was another chance I didn't want to take. In my twisted room we could all continue to pretend that it was nothing more than a pleasant family visit in the bughouse.

I concluded the visit with assurances that I was indeed fine, and, what's more, I'd be out of there soon. That accomplished, I stood and walked them to the double doors.

It was good of them to visit, but if they stayed much longer, things might become uncontrollably weird, for all of us. I hadn't recovered from having forgotten their names. It was better to say good-bye before I started speaking in tongues or clawing at my face or blabbing about the local black market in mirror shards.

After the doors closed behind them, I watched them walk down the hall. Before they turned the corner, Kelly looked back, saw me, and waved. I waved back.

The headache that had been lying in wait exploded across the back of my skull. It started at the base, crawled forward over the top, then drilled straight through my brain like a dozen burning awls, until it reached my eyes.

God damn.

I reached up and rubbed my forehead, though I knew that wouldn't help. I'd been holding the explosion off since the moment I saw Bob Redden coming down the hallway. *I'm not here because I'm crazy, no, of course not.*

Head bowed in a futile attempt to ease the howling pressure, I went back to my room. I wanted to lie down. Exhaustion flooded over me, seeping from my burning head through my arms and legs. The strain of having to deal with regular people, of having to behave like them, knowing I was being closely observed all the while, sucked the energy out of me. Even the light was hurting my eyes.

Before I crawled into bed, though, I had to do something about those flowers. I had to get rid of them. I grabbed the vase off the nightstand and considered dumping it in the trash. A better idea came to mind.

I carried the vase to the nurses' station and set it on the counter.

"Here," I said to the nurse on duty, whose name, I remembered, was Maddie. "You can have these. Brighten the place up a bit."

"They're beautiful!" she sang. "You don't want them? Are you sure?"

"No, no—I'm real sure. They might be full of rats, and even if they aren't, they'll find a way to kill me anyway."

Her face fell, just as I realized exactly what I had said. Mr. Lacan would have explained that as a symptom of something, too. All I know is, talking is a habit I will break myself of one of these days.

"Did I just say that?" I pressed on my right temple with one hand. "Jesus, I'm real sorry, Maddie—I don't know where the hell that came from. Just this damned headache."

"It's okay." She took the flowers, examining them before sliding them a few feet away from me.

"Say." I leaned my elbows on the counter. "I don't suppose I could get a couple aspirins, could I? This thing's not going away."

Maddie glanced over her shoulder. "I really should check this out with the doctor first," she whispered. "You're not on any other meds?"

"No."

"Then I guess it'll be okay."

"Great, thanks."

She looked around quickly, then popped open a bottle behind the counter and shook two tablets into her hand. "Any word on who's handing out the mirror?"

Did everybody know?

"No, ma'am." She handed me the pills and a paper cup full of water. "Thanks." Was I was being kept here to find out who had the mirror? If that was the case, maybe I should get on it one of these days.

I popped the pills in my mouth and drank the water. When they hit the back of my tongue, I had a flashback to sitting on the floor of my apartment, shoving those grainy, half-dissolved sleeping pills into my mouth with my fingers. That taste. My lips and tongue going numb. The muscles of my throat seized up and closed tight, blocking the aspirin.

Maddie's eyes widened as I gagged.

"Here, let me get you some more water," she offered. The chalky tablets broke apart on my tongue, and their bitter taste filled my mouth, then began sliding toward my throat. It was the same as that night. I screwed up my face, wanting to spit them out. I wouldn't be able to get them down. Maddie handed me a fresh cup. I threw the water back, hoping it would wash the pills down completely before my throat realized what was happening.

This time they got to the top of my throat before getting stuck. I gagged again. I thought I was going to puke, as my guts convulsed. I stopped and breathed deeply, trying to calm my stomach. Working my tongue back and forth, I dredged the two pills back up and into my mouth. I spit them into the empty cup I was holding.

"Jesus," I told her. My eyes watered and my nose was running, my throat was thick with phlegm and bile, and my stomach was still seizing. "Can't get them down." I wiped the tears from my eyes. "Maybe I'll just go take a nap. Maybe that's what I should do, huh?"

Maddie took the cup from me and set it on the countertop. "Have you always had trouble swallowing pills?"

I paused.

If I had any trouble swallowing pills, I wouldn't be here. "Not until now."

I thanked her and turned down the hall. Christ, what an hour. I can't remember the names of my own relatives, my head explodes, I admit my fear of plants to a nurse, and then I find I can't swallow pills. Maybe Mr. Lacan was trying to help me understand his theories from beyond the grave. Maybe the room was working its mojo on me. Maybe the whole place was working its mojo.

At least I knew why I couldn't swallow pills. There

was no mystery to that one. I could put words to that just fine.

I went back to my room and sat down on my bed. For the first time since my arrival, apart from the occasional hint, I had started to forget about sanity. It had never really done me that much good over the years, anyway.

I thought about it: The most interesting people in the world, at least among those I'd met, were less than normal, less than sane. The smartest people, too—those who refused to think like others—were among the insane. The best advice I'd received from a shrink, the first I'd had, back in Madison, was to go out and try to destroy the world. It was sage advice to me at the time, but hardly sane.

Sanity, I realized now, was a distinctly overrated attribute.

One thing I had forgotten, though, as the pounding in my head intensified, the pain reaching down my back and toward my fingertips, was that nobody ever talks about how *painful* madness can be.

"Living there, you'll be free, if you truly wish to be."

My ass.

15. Day Pass

"One of our nurses tells me you had a little trouble last week."

My sphincter tightened. I was feeling warm.

"What . . . uh . . . kind of trouble are you talking about, exactly? I don't remember anything in particular." I knew that, in theory, you weren't supposed to lie to shrinks, but what the hell.

Dr. Spellman leaned back in his chair. He slid my file off the table and held it up to read.

"She says you gave her some flowers or something, a gift a visitor had brought for you, and said there were rats in it, and that they would try to kill you."

Oh, why did she need to do that?

"That's not exactly right," I told him. "First of all, you've got to realize that I had a blinding headache. My mind wasn't thinking too straight. The visitors I'd had made me all nervous and flustered."

"Before I ask why that was, why don't you tell me what you told the nurse?"

I sighed. There was no way to make this sound good.

"I don't know for certain. Something along the lines of, 'There're probably rats in there, and even if there aren't, it'll try to kill me anyway.' "

"The rats?"

"No, the plant."

"The *plant* will try to kill you."

"Right."

He didn't say anything for a long time. I turned to Jason, sitting in the corner, and shrugged.

"So why did you think that? About the plant?"

I sighed again, then decided to try to argue it in Spellman's terms. I knew I was fucked. "Hey, we all have absurd fears, right?" I began. "Some people are afraid of water. Some people are afraid of heights or of flying. Without any real justification."

"They think they might drown, or that the plane they're on might crash."

"My mother's afraid of bridges," I offered.

"Maybe she's afraid she'll drive off the side. What can a plant do to you?"

Weeks before, I'd explained some of my other fears to Dr. Spellman. We'd already had this discussion, in a form. By now I had come to the conclusion that it was none of his goddamn business. My silly fears had nothing to do with why I was in here. Besides, I knew precisely where those phobias came from. I knew how to deal with them. They weren't all that debilitating, anyway. Not terribly.

So long as there were no clowns, garden hoses, or ketchup around. Or plants.

"*Nothing*, okay? Not a *goddamn* thing. It was a *joke*, all right?" The rage I had controlled so well before was slipping loose. I slapped my hands on the table in frustration.

Why is he making a big deal about the plants? He was fine with the clowns and the ketchup when I mentioned them.

I heard movement. I saw Jason standing, looking at us, waiting for the word, ready to pounce.

"Don't worry," I told him, "I'm not going to do anything. I'm just frustrated. You can sit back down." He remained standing, and I turned to Spellman, not thinking that, just maybe, the doctor was actually doing his job. That didn't matter at the time.

"I mean, why do we fear what we fear?" I asked. "Why do we *like* what we *like*? Why does the same piece of music make one person feel good, and make another one want to gouge his own eyes out? It's a question no philosopher or psychologist has ever been able to answer. Not in thousands of years of trying."

"I'm a psychiatrist."

"Fine, it's a question no philosopher, psychologist, or *psychiatrist* has ever been able to answer."

I had Spellman beat. I had read book after book on aesthetics, from the Greeks onward, looking for an answer to that simple question. I'd looked in psychology books as well, and books on biochemistry. Doctors could talk about the endorphin-producing "pleasure center" in the brain, but they couldn't say why simply hearing or looking at something could trigger pleasure. Right? *Ha!* He didn't have an answer for me. If he did, he sure as hell wouldn't be here, sitting in judgment over the Mickey Mouse Club. *Ha!*

My mind raced on toward glorious victory, as Dr. Spellman looked at his watch. "Our time is about up. Is there anything else you'd care to bring up before we quit?"

What I really wanted was an answer to the fundamental question behind the study of aesthetics and human motivation. Better still, I wanted him to admit that he didn't have that answer, then proclaim me the winner of the day. Instead, I blurted out, "Can I have a day pass?"

Spellman stared at me. His face betrayed nothing, no reaction whatsoever.

"A day pass," he said finally. It wasn't a question.

"Yeah."

"Why?"

I let my thoughts slip back into gear, back toward fundamentals. Always start with the basics.

"Well, I haven't been outside in all the time I've been here. I'd like to pick up a few things at my apartment, maybe have lunch someplace. My folks would be with me the whole time—and they aren't about to let me run away."

Spellman flipped idly through my file.

"Do you really think I'm crazy?" I asked.

He didn't say anything.

"I mean, have I ever given you the impression that I was as bad as someone like Gus out there?"

Still no answer.

"Do you think that if you let me outside for a couple hours I'd go hurt somebody or rip off my clothes over on Hennepin and start grabbing people?"

"I don't think that."

During the course of our meetings, brief as they had been, I had told Spellman a few things about myself, figuring that's what he wanted, figuring that's what I needed to do to get myself out of there. I'd never told him anything in depth. How could I, in ten minutes? He didn't know anything that I hadn't told anyone else. While telling him these things, I thought, I'd always handled myself well. I behaved and spoke rationally, never said anything too out of line.

I was being pleasant and cooperative. Which is quite possibly why I was still in there. I was playing along, but at the same time not giving him much of a scrap to go on. That was my fault. I didn't think he deserved to learn anything about me. That would give him too much satisfaction, and give him even more of an advantage than he already had.

"We'll see," Spellman sighed.

"Fine, that's all I ask. Thanks."

"Now our time really is up."

I thanked him again and left.

I spent that afternoon as I had most every other after-noon, waiting and watching. This time, though, I had two new people to watch. Two new patients had arrived on the ward.

There was Chaim, who was three or four years older than I was. He was short, with dark hair, glasses, and a scruffy beard. Initially I wasn't sure what specific mistake he'd made to land himself in here. He was in a perpetual state of giddiness. I'd known a few people on the outside who were always happy. They were annoying, maybe, and I generally thought they were kind of dim, but not crazy. Try to talk to Chaim for a few minutes, however, and it was evident that he had only one foot, or toe, planted—and not all that firmly—in the soil of reason. Among his multiple tics, he ended his sentences with increasingly large numbers.

"Isn't it a great day, four thousand two hundred and sixty-seven?" he'd ask.

"I'll say!" I'd reply.

"Yes, it sure is," he would affirm, "five thousand and twenty-five."

Then there was Jenny, a stout woman in her late for-ties, with short, curly black hair going gray. It was easy enough to determine that she was an obsessive-compulsive. There were plenty of them there. And that was probably the main reason the place stayed so clean.

Jenny would circle the room relentlessly, silently, like a shark, always on the prowl for a chair or an ashtray out of place. Those were the two things she focused on. She'd snatch up any obvious scrap of paper on the floor, but not if she had already homed in on a chair or an ashtray. Whenever anyone stood up, she was there in a jiffy to make sure the chair was pushed in properly. If someone moved an ashtray from its position in the center of a table, she was there to snap it back into place, whether it was being used or not.

A few of the more conscious patients, when they'd become aware of her assumed custodial role, began toying with her. Moving ashtrays inches out of position, empty chairs minutely cockeyed—and giggling all the while— to see how long before she noticed and flew into action to make corrections. It fast became the new sport on the ward, a game that never ended and never bored anyone. By all appearances, Jenny enjoyed it, too. It kept her occupied.

I watched her make her rounds for about an hour that Saturday before I went back to my book. It was a good thing I wasn't keeping a journal. It would've been difficult in the first place, given that I had a pen but no paper. Even if I had had paper, though, page upon page of *"2:46—* Jenny adjusts Jack's ashtray, Jack replaces it where it was. *2:49—*Chaim kicks empty chair at table four, Jenny repositions it . . ." would've caused me nothing but trouble had it been discovered.

At five that evening, I called my parents from the communal telephone at the nurses' station. I wanted to let them know the good news about the pass.

There was one phone on the ward that we patients were free to use, as long as we didn't get all wacky about it, calling strange foreign lands or ordering Indian take-out. It was at the far end of the nurses' station, and a chair had been placed next to it so you could sit down while you chatted. I avoided using the phone for a few weeks, out of fear I might catch something, but I got over that. The patients took the privilege seriously and, for the most part, didn't abuse it. Most had nobody on the outside who wanted to hear from them anyway.

While obvious prank calls weren't much of a problem, imaginary calls were. I had seen and heard people make calls to good friends they had out there who cared about their well-being and were overjoyed to hear from them. They talked and laughed and talked some more, loudly, to guarantee that we all heard. But when the nurses on duty suggested after a half-hour or so that they might want to hang up and give others a chance to use the phone, it was discovered they weren't talking to anyone— just listening to the time or the weather.

Eddie the Paranoid was in the habit of picking up the phone, hitting a few numbers—sometimes he didn't even bother with that—and accusing whoever he imagined was on the other end of any number of things.

"If *you* don't know where my sister is, then *I* sure don't know where she is, either! . . . *What* house number? I don't *know* her *house number!* . . . Call the hospital? Why should *I* do that when it's obviously *your* fault? *All your fault!*"

After a few minutes of this, he'd usually slam the phone down and stomp away, fuming.

"Hey, Dad," I said when my father answered the phone.

"Hey . . . Is everything okay?" His voice was immediately worried.

"No, no—I mean, *yes,* everything's fine. Nothing's wrong."

"That's good. Your mom and I are fine, too."

"Well, that's good. Say, I have some good news."

"You're getting out?" He sounded so hopeful. I hated to disappoint him.

"Well, no, not exactly. Yes and no. I mean, I'm not getting *out* out, but the doctor said I could have a day pass."

"Well, that's great news!" he shouted. "For when?"

I hadn't thought of that.

"Whenever I like," I told him.

I knew that Spellman had said nothing of the sort,

had made no such promise, but I opted to hope for the best, to take his distant hint at the possibility as a simple given, to believe in it so strongly that he could never turn me down. Not with my parents waiting for me, and not with the whole ward believing it, too. He just couldn't.

We decided that Tuesday would be a good day. My parents would come for me about noon, and we'd stop by my apartment and go out to eat and do whatever the hell else we wanted to do. It would be a great day.

I started spreading the word the next morning. When I told Chaim that I had gotten a day pass, he said, "Yeah, me too. I got a day pass forever and ever and ever. Eighty-five thousand sixteen."

One day, yes, I hoped to understand what it was he was counting, but I had my doubts that I ever would. I was still working on Gus, without much progress.

A few patients I told congratulated me. Some asked to come along. Only Eddie was pissed at the idea. "I know what you're up to." He hissed behind me while we were all gathered around the lunch cart.

"What's that, Eddie?" I turned and asked.

"Oh, I *know* what you're up to." He slipped in front of me, snatched his tray off the cart, and vanished.

On Tuesday, my parents showed up at about eleven o'clock. While my mom waited down the hall as usual, my dad came in to get me. I ran to my room and put on a rust-brown pullover that my mom had brought a few weeks earlier. Though I could see through the big picture windows that it had been an easy winter so far for Minneapolis—no major blizzard to date—there was still plenty of snow on the ground.

I remembered the storm that had left most of the snow there. Not a blizzard the way I'd come to know them, just a good, heavy snow that fell for two days. I had sat in my chair and watched it blow around, thick and white. I felt the same tickle of joy I'd felt as a kid in Wisconsin when the snow began to fall. Then it had meant the promise of adventure. Sledding in the park until I couldn't feel my feet anymore, building incompetent snow forts in the backyard. Here, though, as I sat in this wide, quiet room, with no wind, no chill, no one else bothering to notice the snow, and realized it didn't promise anything, the tickle faded into a slow ache, then nothing at all. It was distant and alien and useless, like a video of logs burning in a fireplace. Now the snow was beginning to disappear; before, with the drifts, it would've come up to a man's waist or higher.

I went to meet my dad at the front desk, where he was talking to one of the nurses on duty—and where Eddie the Paranoid had seen fit to sneak up on him. My father, a twenty-six-year Air Force vet, either didn't notice, or chose to ignore the fact that Eddie was standing so close behind him, staring at the back of his head. I sneaked up behind Eddie—who was too involved in staring to notice me— and tapped him on the shoulder. He whipped around.

"Eddie, go away," I said. "He knows everything there is to know about you. He won't help." Eddie slunk back toward the television room, glaring accusations over his shoulder as he went.

"Hi," I brightly greeted the nurse behind the desk. It wasn't Maddie the snitch, mercifully. "On Saturday, Dr. Spellman told me I could have a day pass. So we'd like to head out now, please." I had nothing more to say to her.

"Okay . . ." The nurse squinted at me briefly and glanced at my father. "The doctor didn't mention anything about this, but let me check your file."

My guts sank just as Gus erupted behind us.

"FIVE STOPS! FIVE GODDAMN STOPS! FUCK! I'M NEVER GOING TO GET THERE! HITLER STOPPED FIVE GODDAMN TIMES!"

My father and I turned and watched until Gus resumed his normal muttering. By this time, I had become desensitized to his outbursts. I heard them, of course, and was interested that this one was off schedule, but my dad had never had the privilege before. He looked at me, confused and concerned.

"Don't worry about him," I said quietly, as my dad stared again at Gus. "He's harmless. He just yells funny things." I had to remember that "five stops" reference; later I'd study how that might fit into the verbal jigsaw that was Gus.

The nurse was returning with my file, looking through it, shaking her head.

"No, I'm sorry. There's nothing here. No mention of being granted a day pass."

In the back of my head, I'd known this would happen. But I'd spent the past three days believing so firmly that it wouldn't that hearing those words was like having my head slammed in a car door. Rage ripped through me.

They can't do this to me.

I planted my hands on the counter, as I had on Spellman's table, leaned in close, and hissed at the nurse. "The doctor *told* me that I could have a *day pass.* The two of us *talked* about it on *Saturday."* The nurse slowly stepped back a few feet, out of reach.

I looked up at my dad, who was now staring at me, fear and sadness across his face. For the first time, I saw, he was convinced that I really was nuts. Irretrievably, hopelessly mad. I was as mad as Gus over there.

Shit.

My father had never seemed so disappointed. This look now was even worse than the one he'd given me at my high school graduation, when, in protest of something or another, I refused to stand for the national anthem. I was the only one who didn't. It even outranked the look he gave me after he found out I had slit my wrists wide open. He'd been heartbroken both times, but had never appeared this devastated. That stopped me. I took a breath.

"Okay. I'm very sorry," I said, turning back to the nurse, who was about to signal Jason and his thugs over to take care of this situation. "I didn't mean to lose my temper—it's just that I've been locked in here for so long . . . and Spellman told me that I could have a day outside, get some air, move around a little, you know?"

The nurse closed my file.

"I was just looking forward to it so much."

"Tell you what"—she was visibly calming down herself—"I'll give the doctor a call right now, and see what he says."

"That's fair enough. That'd be swell." I smiled as warmly as a person who was fighting the urge to jump over the counter to strangle her with a phone cord could.

She disappeared into a back office, and I looked at my dad. He was still silent, still staring at me with hopeless eyes.

"I shouldn't've lost my temper. I just wasn't expecting any trouble with this, is all."

"It'll be fine." He clapped one of his huge hands on my shoulder. "If we can't go today, we'll go some other day. It'll be fine."

"Yeah. I know. It'll be fine."

"Day-pass trouble?" growled a voice next to me. I was startled to see Jack. I couldn't remember seeing him get out of his chair during the day, except at mealtimes or to get his pills and smokes.

"Yeah," I said, "they might be screwing me here."

He took a short pull on his cigarette and let the smoke nestle in his lungs. "Don't worry about it. Nothing new. They do it to everybody. Don't sweat it."

"I know. It's cool."

"It's a test."

"Pardon?"

"It's a *test*," he said a bit more loudly. "See how you react to disappointment." Once he caught sight of the returning nurse, Jack was back in his chair as if he'd never left it.

The nurse smiled as she approached. "The doctor gave his okay. You can have a three-hour pass."

"Three *hours*? But—"

My dad wisely tapped my hand and nodded.

"That would be great. Better than nothing. Thanks for giving him a call."

She filled out a yellow slip with a carbon copy, stating when we were leaving and when we were due back. She had my father and me sign it, and after signing it herself gave me the original to hang on to and paper-clipped the carbon on my file. "There, you're all set. We'll see you back here at three." She smiled again, glad to be rid of me.

"This is great," I said, holding my release, "but there's one thing."

"Yes?" A nervous look returned.

"Do you suppose I could have my shoelaces? I'd hate to go in the snow and ruin my slippers."

The fading stench of stale vomit hit my nose the moment I pushed open my apartment door. My mother saw the wave of distaste cross my face.

"I cleaned up in here a lot," she said. "You'd thrown up on the bathroom floor. I opened the windows a crack to try and air things out a little."

"Thanks," I told her. "I wouldn't've wanted to come home to find that waiting for me." My parents took a seat on the couch while I strolled through the few rooms, peeking into corners and closets.

"I threw the orange juice in the sink away, too," my mom said when I stepped into the narrow kitchen. "It'd gone bad."

"Yeah, I forgot about that," I shouted back. I opened the refrigerator. Not much in there. There never had been. The stainless-steel sink was cleaner than I'd ever seen it. She must have scrubbed it. That and the stovetop. I was amazed to discover it really was white.

Everything was in place. Everything was neat and clean, except for the smell. That didn't bother me too much, though, after a few months on the ward, where there were no smells, if you forgot the acrid cigarette smoke. Even the dinner cart didn't smell like anything.

On the ward, fluorescent lights were always glaring down. There were no shadows to speak of, except near the television set. The sounds were forever the same— muttering voices, shuffling feet. Cigarette smoke filled your nostrils and strangled off anything that might try to sneak into your nasal passages. The meals were the same, day after day, and none had any taste (not that I minded).

Lights, sounds, smells—they were like the days themselves: always the same, unchanging, eternal.

Being in the ward was like being no place at all. Enough time in there, and the outside world could seem like a terrifying distant planet. The movement of traffic and people, the noise—of voices, laughing, screaming, of car horns, radios, footsteps, crunching snow—it was almost too much, after all those weeks of nothing.

I looked around the apartment for a few more minutes, and out the window at the brick wall across the alleyway; I took in what I could, remembered too much, then told my folks I was ready to go. It was beginning to close in on me again; I couldn't stand quietly in the apartment without recalling the taste of the pills on my tongue. This was the last thing I had expected. My stomach cramped up on me. I had to get out before I puked.

"Are you sure?" my dad asked. "Did you want to bring anything back with you?"

"Just my hat and coat. Maybe I'll be able to use them soon." I reached up on the bookshelf by the door, where my tattered, stained black fedora was sitting on top of a pile of Céline and Kafka. I clamped it on my head. It still felt right. I took my trench coat off the hook on the wall and slipped it on. That felt right, too. "Maybe I'll be needing these again soon, huh?"

They both smiled sadly at me, letting me repeat myself. I'd been repeating myself far too often these past weeks. Probably the result of not having anyone listen to what I was saying anymore, or the strangeness of hearing my own voice, given how rarely I actually spoke. Repeat yourself too often in front of a normal, and you'll end up in the nuthouse.

"C'mon, let's go get something to eat," I suggested. I hoped my stomach would calm down once I got out of the apartment.

When we reached the sidewalk outside, I stopped.

"I'd like to take a walk around the block before we go, just by myself, if that's okay." My parents glanced at each other nervously. My dad had promised the nurse that they'd keep an eye on me at all times. I knew it sounded bad the moment I said it.

"We should come along," my dad answered. I winced, but not too visibly. I knew he would say that. He had to.

"Okay." I'd wanted to prove to my parents that I wasn't insane, that I was responsible enough to take a quick walk around my own block, but their fear was understandable. I wanted to stretch my legs and get some real air in my lungs before I went back into captivity.

The neighborhood hadn't changed much since I'd been away, except for the snow. The trees were about as bare as they were in November, the sidewalks were still broken, and no buildings had vanished or burned down. There was still a mailbox on the corner. Looking toward downtown, I could see the blue glass IDS tower poking into the clouds. The tallest building in Minneapolis, it had been featured in the title sequence of *The Mary Tyler Moore Show;* it was the first landmark that had been pointed out to me after I moved here, and remained the only one I recognized.

The day was cool and wet. I filled my nostrils with the clean gray air and felt the drizzle cling to my hands and face. I had no desire to run away. I wasn't going to try to convince my parents to drive me to Wisconsin that afternoon. But it did feel mighty nice to breathe again. It even felt good to slip on the remaining thin patches of ice and to trip over cracks in the sidewalk.

When we got back to the car, I took a last look at my building. It was nothing special: a squat three-story red brick rectangle, nondescript to anyone passing by.

"You're sure you don't need anything more?" my dad asked.

"Nah, it's not like I'm moving into the ward. I'll be out in the blink of an eye." I said that mostly for their benefit. It was easier to do away with my own hopes and deal with the situation as it rolled on, day after day. The way things were going with Spellman, and the way the nurses were conspiring, the little fuck-ups I kept stumbling into, the less energy I had to care.

We got into the car and I looked back again. My apartment was waiting for me, and sometime I might—I would—be able to call it home again. Yet after those unnerving minutes in it today, I didn't know what was best.

We went to a diner for lunch, and I ordered things I

hadn't tasted in months—a cheeseburger and a beer. The beer went straight to my head. Everything on my plate had flavor and texture. The conversation centered on family news and what I'd do when I got out. But it stopped dead cold when it reached the doors of the ward.

Mom and Dad had heard and seen enough about that place. We didn't need to talk about it when I wasn't there. Out here, we could pretend that I was a respectable citizen, leading a regular life, and that they had come up for an ordinary visit. We could go where we wanted; we weren't constrained by locked doors or the watchful eyes of an orderly. When lunch was over, though, it was time to go back to reality.

Saying good-bye was tough, much tougher than when they had come to see me in the ward. After those three hours of pretending, they had to return me. I'd have to check back in like a criminal, hand over my yellow slip, resume my role as one of the nation's mentally unstable and potentially dangerous.

Those last few blocks back to the hospital, none of us said a word.

16. *f ü n f*

When I awoke, I was inside a bus terminal. A blizzard was raging outside. My parents were gone, but I was still strapped in the wheelchair, holding a bus ticket. There were twenty or so other passengers in the terminal, all milling about, waiting to board. An announcement came over the public address system, so garbled that I had no idea where I might be headed. There was no indication on the ticket. But there seemed to be only one bus out, and I assumed it was mine.

Because I was in a wheelchair, I was let on first, and installed midway toward the back, in a space next to a big window. I was still covered with a blanket, but now, with the blizzard, I was glad to have it. Then I realized something peculiar about the passengers getting on after me.

I could recognize them—Steve, Grinch, old friends from high school, other students from the university— but they were all wearing terrible disguises. Grinch was dressed in Hasidic black, with ear ringlets glued to the inside of his hat. Steve was dressed like a Pilgrim, with buckle shoes and a tall wide-brimmed hat. They shot me quick looks as they boarded the bus, as if I wasn't supposed to recognize them.

Out the window, I saw Elaine again, standing by the terminal doors, wearing a wedding dress. She was smiling and talking calmly with her parents as wind whipped the heavy snow around them. Steve hopped off the bus and went to talk with them, holding tight to his tall hat. He said something to Elaine and touched her lightly on the arm. She turned and stared at me, then looked away.

I was to be the subject—object?—of some sort of surprise party.

Elaine got on the bus, followed by Steve. The driver pulled the door shut with a squeal and started the engine. Elaine's parents waved good-bye, and we rolled off into the snow. There was a mechanical click and hum. I looked outside, just as large wings slid into position on either side of the bus. A moment later we were airborne. I kept watching out the window and saw the terminal spinning away beneath us until it was lost in the storm.

Inside the bus, everyone whispered and looked curiously in my direction. A cluster of old women, or at least people dressed like old women, surrounded Elaine.

The bus was airborne for maybe forty-five minutes. Because of the storm we'd been flying through, it was impossible to determine what city we were landing in—until we touched down in a parking lot and pulled up to the huge glass doors of the terminal. I read the name above the doors: O'Hare International Airport.

Everyone disembarked, leaving me for last. Without a word, Steve climbed aboard and unfastened the belts and locks and straps holding my chair in place, then wheeled me out, across the wide sidewalk and through the sliding glass doors, following the others into the terminal lobby.

It was enormous, with high, skylit ceilings, glass-walled shops, and deep-red carpeting. We were the only people there. Silently, Steve wheeled me past the others to an escalator that led up to what appeared to be another glass wall.

At the top of the escalator, I faced a huge toy store. Toys of all kinds were piled in mountains that nearly reached the ceiling. No aisles, no shelves, only a big jumble of toys. I looked to my right, and discovered that I was parked next to a checkout counter with a variety of candies on display.

What's more, without my noticing, my wheelchair had been transformed into a wooden boat—a small, polished oak speedboat—with a complex set of lights, buttons, and controls on the dashboard.

Distorted calliope music began playing on the other side of the glass, inside the toy store. From behind one of the piles of toys, Mongo—a three-hundred-pound Pakistani, a fellow I had known while at the University of Chicago—rocked his bulk into view, clutching a six-foot-tall inflatable Godzilla in front of him. I saw Steve on top of another mountain of toys with an identical inflatable Godzilla. A voice boomed over the music that a surprise was waiting for me—*if* I could figure out how to make the boat move.

My eyes searched the dashboard. There were no keys, no obvious ignition buttons. But there were three rectangular indentations on top of the control panel, all of different sizes. The largest was roughly five by three inches. I reached to the candy counter and grabbed a handful of candy bars and tried pushing them into the indentations.

From below me, the crowd on the ground floor cheered and shouted out suggestions. I raced through combinations of candy bars as fast as I could, sweating, panicking, not knowing how much time I had, about to give up hope, already wondering what my next strategy should be.

Then, with the final possible combination of candy bars, something clicked. A small engine chugged to life, the lights on the dashboard twinkled, and the toy store split in two, like a game-show set, each half pulling back to reveal what lay beyond.

At first it seemed nothing more than the other half of the terminal lobby, with a smooth, narrow track instead of an escalator leading down to the ground. At the bottom stood my friend Laura's father (whom I'd seen only in pictures) and Laura herself in a wedding dress, holding a rose. Elaine in a wedding dress had been nothing but a cheap ruse.

The boat rolled slowly down the incline, and when it hit the bottom, I reached out my hand to Laura, who took it and climbed in next to me. She handed me a lacquered wooden plaque on which was inscribed a poem, in her handwriting. My eyes raced over the poem; it seemed to indicate that we not only were getting married but were going to take a long trip afterward (*"I want to be with you in Amsterdam and Spain"*). My eyes filled with tears. All I could offer her were three candy bars.

We waved good-bye to the people who had gathered around Laura's father, and moved forward. The track we were on led to a small cave in the middle of the red-carpeted floor. Once inside, we dipped down and headed deeper yet—into what I believed to be a series of secret caverns hidden beneath Green Bay's Downtowner Motel. We splashed into an amusement-park river that ran in an oval. In front of us and behind were several other boats, someone's wedding party (though not ours).

Inside the oval was a craggy island with a small mountain, too big to see over. To the outside, around the entire oval, were regularly spaced brightly lit open door-ways. Most of the light in the cavern came from there; other light came from tiki lamps set up along the island shore.

Boats pulled up to the outside of the oval, and the occupants got out and ran through the illuminated door-ways. I decided that the women with the men were prostitutes after one, obviously drunk, stumbled out of a doorway, crashed onto our boat, and started pawing at me. Laura rolled her off the boat and into the shallow river.

We cruised around, again and again and again, not saying much, content, happier than we'd been in a long time. About the sixth time around, I heard a commotion from one of the rooms. I couldn't see anything when I looked that way, and when I turned back Laura had vanished.

I stood up unsteadily in the boat and shouted for her. She must be on the island, I thought; if she had gone the other way I would have seen her. I shouted more loudly, looking frantically as the boat carried me around the island twice more. Finally, I beached the boat and climbed ashore.

The island was a pocked and ragged black rock. There were a few other people on it. I climbed up the mountain and found Laura silhouetted against a glowing orange backdrop. It looked like sunset, but couldn't have been, because we were underground. She was wearing Wagnerian operatic garb, embracing a large man with red hair and a long red beard, dressed like a lumberjack. The wind was blowing. I no longer knew what I was wearing. Quietly, music started. I recognized it as the first long, slow notes from *Tristan und Isolde.*

She's not dressed for Isolde, I remember thinking. *She's a Valkyrie.*

I started to sing.

"Westwärts . . . schweift der Blick . . . ostwärts . . ."

Then Laura and the lumberjack began to sing, too. Soon they stopped, and I sang the rest of the opera alone, all the parts, standing there at the top of the hill with what appeared to be a glorious orange sunset surrounding me now.

Laura came and embraced me after I was finished, explaining that she was just saying good-bye to the lumberjack. His name was Tom. I told her that if she still loved him, she should stay with him, because I wouldn't be able to live with myself—or her—knowing she'd rather be someplace else.

She couldn't make up her mind, and I got nervous. I mean, I was just being gallant. I didn't really expect it to be a problem. But it was. Tom, who seemed like a nice gentleman, proposed that he and I have a contest, a battle of sorts.

That doesn't sound like a good idea at all. He's three times my size, it's nightfall, and I'm as graceful as a wildebeest.

It wasn't going to be a test of strength, he reassured me, but rather a test of magical wills.

That sounds even worse.

Two dolls appeared on the ground between us—one of Tom, one of myself. We took up positions on either side of them, and then, on the top of that small and quite probably manmade mountain, they began to fight each other like humans, while we controlled their movements with our minds. Each doll was as strong as our respective individual wills to win; physical size was irrelevant.

The battle went on for some time, the dolls throwing each other around, pinning each other, flying at each other, taking a savage beating that no human could withstand, yet remaining more nimble than any human could ever be.

Tom and I began to sweat. We were on our hands and knees, getting closer to the action. My doll caught Tom's with an unexpected trip, and his doll slid over an embankment, toward a precipice and certain death. As Tom's doll slid, mine chased him, and just as his doll went over the edge, mine grabbed its arm and held on.

Slowly, very slowly, my doll pulled him back to level ground. The fight was over. Tom conceded.

He walked over to me and shook my hand. He gave Laura a light kiss on the lips. Then he hopped on a horse, which had appeared from out of nowhere, as had the regiment of armored soldiers behind it.

"On to Valhalla and greater adventures!" Tom cried, kicking his horse into action. He charged over the top of the hill and vanished.

When I went over to Laura, tears were streaming down her face. I told her she could follow him. I'd wait. She kissed me on the cheek and ran over the hill after him.

I sat down and waited and watched the river.

17. Even God Doesn't Like You

My parents were gone. And now Edna was, too.

When I was buzzed through the doors after my three-hour constitutional, she wasn't sitting motionless in her regular spot just inside the doors. I had come to rely on Edna as our sentinel, the guardian of the gates. Without her there, with that sad couch sitting empty, who would protect us?

I stared at the vacant and lonely couch, and scrolled through the logical possibilities. Had she finally made it out? After all these months, perhaps years, had Edna been fooling everyone—was she honing her timing to perfection, so she could zip out the doors before they clicked shut, disappear down the hallway to the elevators and then up, up to illicit freedom? Had someone been foolish enough to discharge her into the world, while I had to be satisfied with a lousy three-hour pass? Had the final inmate uprising taken place without me? Had Edna died? Maybe she'd swallowed her mascara. Or maybe she'd gotten her hands on some of those mirror shards.

More horrifying still than any of these possibilities was one remaining question. With Edna gone, would one of us have to assume her role as the still and silent guardian on the couch?

These questions conga-lined through my head as I stepped into the day room, where I found most of my answers.

Edna was sitting on the floor, her back to the wall, in the corner by Gus. She was staring emptily, her eyes no less dazed than usual, her makeup the familiar jumble of colors and dark designs. She was rocking in light rhythm with Gus's pedaling legs.

Well.

I headed to my room to take off my coat. As I passed the nurses' station, someone called me.

"Jim, wait." I looked. It was Mrs. Cartwright. Funny—I hadn't seen her since my first day.

"Yeah?"

"Hold on there for just a moment, please."

"Okay." I stood where I was, waiting, looking out the window, breathing in the smoke from a dozen burning cigarettes. She came out from behind the counter.

"Hello, Ms. Carmichael."

"Cartwright."

"Yes, I'm sorry." *Nice move, ass-wipe.* "What can I do for you?"

"I have to follow you." She seemed vaguely annoyed.

I guess I'd drawn her away from the mythical on-call doctor and their back-room canasta tourney. Maybe she'd been reading pornography, or knitting.

"Okay." An immobile crazy lady was mobile again, and now a woman I hadn't seen in months wanted to follow me. Maybe the immediate contrast with the outside made it feel so peculiar.

I walked to my room with Ms. Cartwright trailing directly behind me. I opened the door and stepped inside.

I turned to face her. "Yes?"

"If you could hand me your coat, please?"

"Are you going to hang it up for me?"

"Eventually." She was wearing a pantsuit identical to the one she'd been wearing the first time I saw her, except this one was gray. Everything else about her was unchanged: same hair, same frozen eyes. As I slipped my arms free of the trench coat, I squinted at her, trying to read her face. Something seemed amiss.

"What's wrong?"

"Nothing," she said, as she took my coat. "You were outside. Whenever a patient comes back, we have to make sure they aren't carrying any contraband in with them. You understand. You'll need to empty your pockets, please, and please remove your shoelaces again."

She searched the pockets of my coat and felt through the lining, as I sat on the bed and started unlacing my shoes.

Well, I suppose I'd go through pretty much the same thing at any airport.

Satisfied that I wasn't carrying a gun or a knife or a loop of piano wire in the coat, Ms. Cartwright hung it in the closet for me. "Now the hat," she said. I plucked it off my head, handed it to her, and dumped the shoelaces on the countertop. I put the contents of my pants pockets there as well, and she found nothing new or especially interesting.

"Very good, then," she told me. "Thanks for cooperating."

"I wouldn't want to end up in the Time-Out Room, if you know what I mean."

"Mm-hmm," she said, without any apparent meaning. "Has anyone offered you broken glass since you've been here?"

Not again.

"No. Look, everybody's been asking me that. No. *No,* okay? If I see anyone flashing pieces of mirror around, I'll let you know, okay? But believe me, you might as well give up—at least on the notion of anyone telling me. I don't see that happening. Nobody here much deals with me or even talks to me. Nobody's going to tell me a thing."

"Fine," she replied coldly, "but if you do hear anything, please—"

"I'll let you know." After that first night, I hadn't heard the slightest hint that a patient had done anything with mirror shards. None of the folks from the day room had mysteriously vanished, and no one had appeared one morning swathed in bandages. When would these people come to the conclusion that the threat was gone? And why did they keep hassling me about this?

Ms. Cartwright turned and left. I refilled my pockets, put my hat back on, and went to the day room.

"Hey, Jack."

Jack was sitting at his regular table, almost obscured by a cloud of smoke. He was attacking his cigarette the way a hungry man might go after a waffle.

"Yeah, hey," he managed between puffs.

"Miss anything while I was gone?"

"Edna moved."

"I saw that."

"We all watched."

"I can imagine." Edna and Gus must've been staring at each other longingly across the room all this time, none of us suspecting a thing, until she finally decided to do something about it.

"Yeah."

We sat in silence for a while, Jack sucking his cigarette down until it sizzled the flesh between his knuckles. He showed no reaction, then dropped the butt in a half-full black plastic ashtray. The yellow fingers on his battered right hand were covered in scar tissue and cigarette burns. I chose not to say anything, figuring he knew about it well enough already. I tried to picture him on the outside, but couldn't get any further than seeing him sitting at a bar, doing exactly the same thing he was doing here, but with a beer in front of him.

"That's a funny hat," he finally said.

"I like it. It keeps me company."

"Yeah, I used to think things like that, too."

I knew Jack used to talk to electricity—he'd let that much slip—but he never mentioned talking to articles of clothing before. He reached into his shirt pocket and pulled out another cigarette, stuck it in his mouth, and lit it off the butt still smoldering in the ashtray.

Then it struck me, almost casually: Where was Jack getting his smokes? It had been a while since I'd seen him stand in line with the others, but he seemed to have an endless supply. Though he always got one from the nurses when he went for his Haldol, that was only three times a day. Yet I never saw him without a cigarette in his hand.

"Tell me, Jack," I started, as smoothly as possible, "where do you get your cigarettes?"

He took a long drag and snorted the smoke out of his nostrils. "Here."

"Yes, I know 'here.' But how come you always have what you need right there, right on you?"

He took another drag and said, more softly, "I think you know that."

I looked over at the nurses' station. The two nurses I could see were whispering to each other and giggling, paying no mind to the day room.

Had I just stumbled into it? Jack was certainly with it enough to keep things quiet. He kept to himself and seemed trustworthy, and so passive that no one would ever suspect him. Trading shards for cigarettes, that's what they said someone had been doing.

Nobody else seemed to have noticed that Jack had this endless supply of smokes. What was he after with all this? What the fuck was going on with the nurses? They lit his first one every morning; didn't they notice him sitting there all day, puffing away without their assistance?

"Jack, why?" I whispered, leaning in conspiratorially.

He shuffled his chair a few inches and leaned away from me. He never looked at people, never liked people getting too close. I was making a big assumption here, leaping over the rules of scientific inquiry. After all, maybe he won the cigarettes playing checkers. Even if I'd never seen him playing checkers.

He turned his big white head slowly toward me. His eyes never strayed from the tabletop.

"It's like having a part of that other place, the one you were in." Jack nodded toward the picture window and the expanse of the Metrodome outside. He left it at that, but it wasn't enough for me. I wasn't even sure what the hell he meant. I'd try a different tack.

If Jack was the mirror-shard culprit, there was no way

I could turn him in. I don't know that I could have done that to any of these people. Maybe Eddie the Paranoid—I'd gladly have gotten rid of him. I looked around the room, and saw Eddie sitting alone at a table, staring at Jack and me. What if he knew what we were talking about? Right. He probably thought we were Masons.

"You ever heard of Ed Gein?" I asked Jack, as Jenny swung past, pausing long enough to slide the ashtray an inch to the left before moving on.

Jack shook his head. He dropped another burning butt in the ashtray and pulled out a fresh cigarette.

"He lived alone on a farm in Wisconsin, watched people's kids for them every once in a while, brought over packages of venison when he had extra. He was what people called a nice guy, a real quiet guy. Good-neighborly type."

Jack said nothing.

"Funny thing about the venison, though—the guy was never a deer hunter."

I paused.

"One day—back in 1957—he was arrested for the murder of a local woman named Bernice Worden."

Jack remained still except for his cigarette hand.

"She worked at the local hardware store. That's where she was apparently shot to death, but her body disappeared. Anyway, everyone in town was real shocked when they heard later that Ed was arrested for the murder. Like

I said, they all thought he was a nice guy. A little slow, but nice."

I kept watching Jack's downturned face for any sign of recognition. He was old enough to remember, and if he'd always lived around Minneapolis, he must've heard about the Gein case. Hell, it made national news. Even *Life* magazine.

"Well, shocked as people were when they heard that he'd been arrested, they were even *more* shocked when they heard what the police found when they went out to search his house."

Nothing.

"Out in the barn, they found Bernice Worden. She was strung up from the rafters and dressed out like a deer. Her head was gone, and she was split open and all cleaned out. When they went *inside* the house, they found body parts everywhere. There were heads on the bedposts, and skins in the closet, and buckets filled with . . . well . . . other things. Some people say they found a heart in a saucepan on the stove."

I began to consider the insanity of what I was doing. But I had my reasons.

"Turns out that Ed really, really loved his mother. A lot more than most people. He'd always lived with her. And after she died, he didn't want to let her go. So what he was doing was, he wasn't just killing people, like the woman in the store. No sir, he was going out to the cemetery and *digging people up*—women who'd recently died—and *skinning* them, and taking whatever other parts he needed, because he was trying to make himself a woman suit. You ever see the movie *Psycho?*"

Jack reached for another cigarette.

"You should. It's a good movie," I said. "They'd probably never show it to us in here, but it might be on the TV sometime."

I was losing my train of thought. I knew the case backward and forward. Even though it took place eight years before I was born, since I'd grown up in Wisconsin, there was no escaping it.

"Eddie's gonna get you" was a common threat used on naughty children. Older kids dressed up as Gein on Halloween. Most of the local punk bands had at least one song about him in their repertoire.

When I was in high school, I became friends with Judge Robert Gollmar, the kindly white-bearded man who presided over Gein's second sanity hearing, in the sixties. Gollmar wrote a book about the case, *Edward Gein: America's Most Bizarre Murderer.* The judge and I remained friends until his death.

When I was in college in Madison, I lived just off the shores of Lake Mendota, one of the three big lakes bordering the city. Walk out onto the porch of my building, and there, about a mile away, across the short end of the lake, deep in the bowels of the Mendota Mental Health

Center, sat Ed Gein. When news of his death broke in 1985, the newspapers made a big to-do about his burial in an unmarked grave in the Center's graveyard. Which, of course, put the nut in my head that my pal Grinch and I should go dig him up. The place was too close *not* to do it—hell, we could walk there.

Once we got to the Center, though, we found that the security arrangements were a bit beyond our means, so we went back to town and forgot about it. No matter, really, because just two weeks later, in accordance with Gein's wishes, the authorities dug him up, and buried him next to his mother. Irony be damned.

I went on for some time with the story, filling Jack in with the gruesome details—about Gein's attempt to keep the spirit of his mother alive by dressing up in the skins of dead women, and about my own long-term fascination with him. Jack never looked up or gave any indication that he was listening. My plan was to squeeze some reaction out of him, some admission. By telling him about a nice, quiet man who'd done some dreadful things, been caught, and sent to an asylum, I was hoping to spark something, open the doors into Jack's own naughty business.

I wasn't sure it would work, but it was all I could think of at the time, short of just coming right out and asking him for a piece of broken glass, should he have a spare handy. When I had exhausted my horrific Gein tales, I asked him, "Well, what do you think about that, huh?"

Jack worked at his smoke.

"I see why people think you're the worst one here."

"Pardon?"

"You're crazy."

"No I'm not." This wasn't going well.

"Why haven't you got a new roommate yet?" he asked in a phlegmy rumble. "You show up. Joey gets cut. You never get another roommate. Makes sense. Go around telling crazy stories.

"I'm not saying it. Just repeating it," Jack continued. His hands were shaking. "They think you gave him the glass. Some people think you cut him yourself."

"They think *I'm* the one with the mirror?"

"That's what they say."

"I can't tell you how wrong that is. If I'm the one handing out broken mirror, why's the staff here bugging me to find out who's doing it?" I'd kept Jack appraised of my dealings with the administration. I had to tell someone, and of all the patients, he was the most likely to keep it to himself.

"Why do you think they think you're it?" he grumbled. "Everybody thinks you're pretty damn crazy. Always reading that same book."

"It's a hard book."

"Even them." Jack nodded in the direction of Darin and Peter. They were playing an improbable card game three tables away, out of earshot.

"When they first showed up, both of them, they tried

to make us think they were killers or something like that. Nobody believed it—look at them—and when nobody paid any attention, they quit. They only talk to each other." Jack's hands were shaking even more now. He glanced at the clock, then looked back down at the table.

"So," I whispered, "if everyone thinks I've got the mirror, why hasn't anyone asked me for some?"

" 'Cause they think you're a snitch, too. You'll turn 'em in for asking."

"Oh, Lord."

"Please stop speaking of the Lord in such a way."

"Sorry. Look—"

Jack pushed his chair back, stood up, and walked to the nurses' station. I had no idea what was going on. I kept an eye on the nurse and on Jason in the corner, and on Jack at the counter; I was waiting for him to point at me. The nurse turned and walked out of sight.

She's getting the doctor. He's told them that I confessed. I'm in it now, even if I don't have anything on me or in my room. That's why I was given the secret tour—they hoped that the sight of the ECT room would scare the broken glass up and out of me.

The nurse returned and handed Jack a paper cup. He took it in his shaking hands and threw the contents back. Then he took another cup from her and threw that back, too. He nodded slowly and solemnly. He had her light a new cigarette, then came back to his seat.

"You okay?"

"Medicine," he grunted.

"Feeling better?" I asked.

"I will."

I was afraid I'd lost him. If you kept Jack talking, he could go for hours about a single subject. Break his concentration in any way—Gus letting us know what was on his mind, the television room door opening, someone dropping an ashtray or skipping past—and you could lose that conversation forever. I tried to pick up where we'd left off.

"Umm, you know I'm not the one with the mirror, right?"

"We both do."

Two tables in front of us, Mary put her head down and sobbed loudly. Her big shoulders shook with the effort. Eddie was staring with his great black eyes.

"Do you know who is?"

Jack looked around the room slowly. Then he looked directly at me for the first time that day, with soft, clear blue eyes. A tiny smile crept into the corner of his mouth.

"I'm hungry," he said. "Dinnertime soon. I'm a good boy. I get apple crisp." His eyes dropped to the table, he brought the cigarette to his lips, and he fell into a silence I knew I would never break.

My heart fell.

"Well, thanks for the chat, Jack. Helps pass the time." I stood and went to my room. Defeated, I picked up my book, then went back out. I took a seat and started read-ing.

I heard someone giggle with anticipation. "This time of day is not a good time of day today. But dinnertime soon. Nine-six-three-nine-eight-four."

"You bet, Chaim," I said. "Dinnertime soon. Apple crisp, huh?" I was glad to see somebody so happy here. Then again, from the looks of him, Chaim might well be this happy in a leper colony on Devil's Island.

I wondered how different a leper colony would be.

"I DON'T LIKE YOU!" Gus screamed from his perch. "NOBODY LIKES YOU! EVEN *GOD* DOESN'T LIKE YOU!"

I'd heard that line before, somewhere, sometime, hadn't I? I couldn't think too hard on it, though. All I could do was shake the idea out of my head and wait for dinner with the rest of them, and catch up on the time lag I felt from my visit abroad.

I let my mind wander, and looked out the window. It was a good, soft winter outside. I wondered why nobody else ever looked out the window much. Then something that Lacan had written about in one of his essays became frighteningly obvious. I'd been a fool not to think about it before; it was, after all, the thesis of the first essay I'd read in that book.

Lacan had a notion that infants, seeing themselves from their own perspective, perceive their bodies as disjointed pieces. Hands, legs, bellies—separate parts floating in space, unconnected. But there is a profound moment of psychological development when the child first recognizes himself in a mirror. For the first time, the body is seen as a unified object, with all the pieces—arms, legs, head—attached and singular.

When the child first recognizes himself *as himself* in a mirror, he also sees himself as others see him. That's the beginning of both subjectivity and alienation. In an instant, the child becomes one body in a world full of bodies. Like everyone else, and at the same time separated from everyone else: Lacan called it "the mirror stage."

I thought about the mirrors I had to deal with—that everyone had to deal with—in this place. The warped, useless stainless-steel mirrors in the bathrooms, and more important, the shattered mirror I was supposed to be hunting down.

Lacan theorized about what happened when a baby saw himself whole in a mirror, but my question now was, What happens to an adult when his internalized mirror—that perception of self everyone carries around inside—gets shattered into a hundred potentially deadly pieces? Does he get broken into a hundred deadly pieces, too? Maybe he returns to that original state, where his body is composed of separate, unconnected pieces. This Lacan fellow might actually be onto something this time. Maybe even something helpful. All I had to do was determine who had the most disjointed personality in the room; who among us was the craziest. Then I remembered what Jack had told me.

I looked out the window again, stared at the Metrodome, and continued waiting for the dinner cart.

1 8 . Mi, So, La

It was early February, and I was bored. Each day was about the same as the day before. The day that followed would be the same as well. Sit at a table. Wait for the meal cart. Play Go Fish with Eddie. Cards and checkers were the only games available on the ward, and those few who played tended to monopolize them just as strictly as Gus monopolized the bike.

Nobody wanted to play with me. Since no one wanted to play with Eddie the Paranoid either, we were stuck with each other. This was always a mistake, yet there I was, sitting down with him again and again.

Go Fish was the only game he knew, and his reactions were as predictable as the days themselves.

"Got any nines?"

"Nope. Go fish. . . . Got any queens?"

While I studied my cards and waited, there'd be an inevitable long silence from his side of the table. I'd eventually look up to find Eddie's glare aimed at me.

"You're lying."

"Oh Christ, Eddie, I am *not* lying to you."

"Then prove it."

"What?"

"Prove it. Prove you're not lying. Show me your cards. You've got nines. You've got *all* the nines. I *know* it."

"Bullshit, Eddie—I'm not showing you my cards. That ruins the whole game."

"You're lying to me, see? Liar."

"Oh, Eddie, just play the damn game."

"No—not with you *lying* to me all the time. About everything. Nines, threes, *everything*."

Moments later, he would slap his cards on the table and stomp away, to glower at me from across the room.

Because I didn't smoke cigarettes and wasn't on any meds, I didn't even have hourly interruptions to look forward to, to measure the time with. I would read Lacan over and over. I'd stare out the window. I'd replay Killdozer and Residents albums in my head. I'd think my way through old movies. I'd chat with Jack.

The issue of glass shards never came up again with him; since no one else had been hurt by a mirror shard, I didn't see the point of getting him in trouble, especially when I had no real evidence. He was the only one I could talk to at any length and with any coherence. I didn't want to blow that. We talked about inconsequentials—weather, Gus, Jack's old job, outdated news.

Occasionally someone would provide a little local entertainment. Mary would start screaming. Gus would let loose with a string of curses aimed at the ghosts who tormented him. Chaim had taken to fondling himself publicly. In a place like this, he could get away with it.

And who could've guessed that so many folks who heard from God on a regular basis would be gathered together into one room as small as this? But God, it appeared, never really had anything interesting to say. Of course, maybe that signified something.

Every Saturday, I told Dr. Spellman that I was good and ready to get out, that I had a job waiting, that I had no desire to kill myself anymore, that I'd never given the folks on the ward a lick of trouble (well, not much at least). In short, I was "normal" enough to function on the outside. And every Saturday, he told me, in the same words, in the tones of the off-screen figures in a Charlie Brown special, that he was convinced my normality was an act, that he was certain I wasn't ready.

That was a problem. What if it was just an act I was putting on for him once a week? All this time. All this dead time. Who knew what had happened, really? Some days I was stone convinced that I was sane as Lincoln; other days I'd find meaning in the arrangement of the items on my dinner tray. I could flip-flop from hour to hour, from lucid to nutty as a jaybird. My own feeble and brief attempts at self-analysis had been fruitless:

Psychoanalysis. Psycho Anal Lysis. The separation of

the mind from the asshole. This is what I must do. Yes, fine, brilliant. But what the hell does THAT mean?

My public slips made it easy for Spellman to keep holding me there. And the longer he held me, the more I questioned my own stability. The frustrated rage that his bland, dismissive responses dredged out of me early on had faded. I'd come to expect his negative responses now. One more regular part of the weekly routine. I was arriving at the conclusion that my initial ecstatic dream was coming true, only it wasn't nearly so ecstatic anymore. I might well be spending the rest of my days here—without ever having won a Pulitzer, without even having to say funny things all the time.

One evening after dinner, I was staring out the dark picture windows. There was nothing to look forward to except going to bed, then getting up the next morning and repeating today's routine. In the distance, I could see city lights, and cars streaming up and down the streets. There was still a world out there, waiting.

Yeah, waiting. But I might never be part of it again. I felt like I'd been long forgotten.

Christ, I may never ride in another automobile again.

I watched the red and white lights.

But you know? I never liked cars much. Never really liked this town, either.

Someone opened the door to the TV room and stepped out. I heard a familiar tune blaring from the television set.

It wasn't the theme to *Sesame Street* and it wasn't the theme to the professional wrestling show—the two favorites on the ward. It was "Oriental Blues," a spritzy ragtime piano number best known as the theme to the old Ernie Kovacs show.

I glanced through the window at the television screen, and sure enough, there it was—a kaleidoscopic shot of a hundred hands playing piano, then a few shots of Kovacs himself, ever-present cigar in his mouth.

My dad had introduced me to Ernie Kovacs during the mid-seventies, when a "Best of" series was shown on PBS. My father had grown up watching Ernie Kovacs, and had gauged my sense of humor enough to think I might appreciate it, too. I did. So much so, in fact, that it led to my participation in wide-scale grade-school playground wars between nerdy Monty Python fans and a new crop of nerdy Ernie Kovacs fans, who had discovered the show when it replaced *Monty Python* on Saturday nights on Green Bay's Channel 38.

I was a Monty Python fan, sure, but Kovacs was different. A lot of his jokes I never got—like the half-hour episode he did without a single spoken word, relying on visuals and sound effects alone to tell us what was going on. He constructed music videos, complete with spinning cow heads, overweight ballerinas, food, and office furniture, to accompany the *1812 Overture* and "Sentimental Journey." Even though I couldn't always grasp why what he was doing was funny, it made me laugh, if a little nervously.

I also liked Kovacs's show because it was something my dad and I could watch together. There wasn't much of that on television when I was growing up, except for the Packers every Sunday.

Now, on the ward, I hesitated. I had pretty much avoided the television room since my arrival. High jinks went on in there. Bad high jinks. And Kovacs's sketches were ultraviolent in a cartoonish, fifties way. They might well have the same effect on these mental cases that the professional wrestling did. There was a chance I'd be set upon, killed, and devoured if I dared cross the threshold.

But Ernie Kovacs would be worth it.

Even if they tore me apart and ate my flesh in a lustful Dionysian frenzy it would still be worth it.

The door to the TV room swung open, and I scanned the area. Six or seven people sitting in the darkness. Dumb, sweaty, expressionless faces picked out by the shifting gray-blue light of the screen.

I took a seat on a couch near the back wall, so my hat (which I wore all the time now, except while sleeping or showering) wouldn't block anyone's view. I stayed close to the door, too, so escape, if necessary, would be simple. A man named Lars sat on the other end of the couch.

Lars was a religious zealot who saw angels and

demons everywhere. Mostly demons. He was large, bearded, blond, and Swedish. He wore thick horn-rimmed glasses, and hospital pajamas and bathrobe all the time, thinking people would take him more seriously as a prophet that way. Lars didn't bother me. He'd once claimed I was a demon, but at one time or another he claimed everyone was a demon.

Lars said nothing when I sat down. Nobody did.

One of Kovacs's more famous characters, Percy Dovetonsils, Poet Laureate, was on the screen pursing his lips, shaking his head, and sipping a martini. Percy was a swishy drunk who wore a garish smoking jacket and read his dreadful poems with a nasal lisp.

Nobody in the room was laughing. I tried to keep my growing chuckles to myself. It wasn't just the show that was making me laugh; the change of pace was making me giddy. I was actually seeing something I *liked.* What's more, nobody was making a move to change the channel or bite me.

"Ernie Kovacs was the funniest, wildest, zaniest man I ever knew," Lars whispered.

I turned and looked at him. He could've been old enough, I supposed. The beard, and right now the shadows, made it hard to determine his age: he could have been anywhere from thirty-five to sixty-five. Lars may well have been one of Kovacs's chief writers, for all I knew.

I leaned over. "You knew Ernie Kovacs?" I asked.

Someone near the front immediately *shhh'*ed. Religious fanatic or not, if Lars knew Ernie Kovacs, I wanted to hear about it.

"Ernie Kovacs was the funniest, wildest, zaniest man I ever knew," he repeated. Nobody shushed Lars, probably because he was a regular. "Ernie thought so, too. And so did millions of happy people. Ernie was all over television from 1950 until he died in 1962—"

It took me a moment to realize that Lars was mimicking the opening to the PBS show. It's what Jack Lemmon read over the credits. *God damn that Lars.* He kept talking, and I wasn't going to try to stop him. The results were usually mighty ugly if he had to struggle to get something out of his system.

"He had an unpredictable and illogical view of the world. He played with the medium of television in a way no one ever had before, and he created a batch of cockeyed characters that have become classics. So slow down your internal clock—it was a more leisurely time, you know."

"I know, Lars," I muttered in frustration. The show's final credits were already rolling.

When they were over, a voice on the television commanded: "Stay put—there's more of *The Best of Ernie Kovacs* coming up next." There was a public television fund-raiser going on. I thought about taking up a collection around the room and calling it in, but soon dismissed the notion: the folks at PBS probably didn't have much use for lint and soiled Kleenex.

Another episode was good news—maybe I'd actually get to hear most of this one—so I stayed tight in my seat. None of the others in the room moved, either.

"*Demon,*" Lars whispered at me just as it got started.

"*Shhh.*" I shot back at him. The same voice in the front *shhh*'ed me in turn, and Lars went on to recite Jack Lemmon's opening bit along with him, word for word, pause for pause.

"Ernie Kovacs was the funniest, wildest, zaniest man I ever knew. . . ."

I ignored him, happy at least that he was getting his recitation out of the way early, and tried to enjoy the show. Near the end of the episode, the Nairobi Trio appeared. Like Percy Dovetonsils, they were Kovacs regulars. They'd disturbed me profoundly when I first started watching the show as a child. I still think they were intentionally unsettling.

The Nairobi Trio consisted of three men in longhaired ape masks, trench coats, gloves, and bowlers, who moved like robots against a black backdrop and mimed a performance of Robert Maxwell's peculiar ditty "Solfeggio." One conducted, one played piano, and one used his drumsticks on the conductor's head. It was all strangely sinister.

As the skit played on, I could feel Lars becoming agitated a few feet from me. He was shifting from haunch to haunch as if he had a bad case of hemorrhoids. Given his size and the fact that he spent all his time on the couch in front of the television, it wouldn't have surprised me. When it finally became too distracting, I turned to him.

"Lars, *what?*"

He looked at me bug-eyed, pointed at the screen, and yelled, *"You're one of them!"* Every head in the room turned away from the screen and looked, too.

"What?"

"You're one of *them! Demon!*"

A few of the others giggled nervously, but there was no mirth in Lars's eyes. They were filled with wild hatred. At first I had no idea what he was talking about, but then it hit me. I had the hair. I had the hat. I had the long, dopey face. A few, maybe even Lars, had seen me wearing the trench coat when I came back from my three hours outside.

I had spent years skulking around darkened alleyways and rain-slick streets in my trench coat and black fedora, convinced that I looked like a film noir character, some tough guy out for trouble, knowing damn well he'd find it if he just waited long enough.

According to Lars, I'd been wrong that whole time.

No sir, I looked like a member of the Nairobi Trio who'd wandered away from the set. No wonder nobody was ever much impressed.

"N-n-n-o demon, Lars," a childlike voice from the front stuttered. "M-m-monkey."

That was all the encouragement the rest of the patients in the room needed.

"*Mon-key! Mon-key! Mon-key! Mon-key!*"

A maniacal, gleeful chant came out of every one of them, and grew in intensity. They were up on their feet now, pointing and waving their arms, hopping about the room, blocking my view of the screen, shouting.

"*Mon-key! Mon-key! Mon-key!*"

I was back in Green Bay, in grade school, in junior high, in high school. It never ends. There's no escape.

Before they had a chance to grab me, I took my hat off and retreated to my own room, head down. I closed the door behind me and lay on the bed. Nobody would bother me here. They were too afraid to come in here, after what happened to Joey. Goddamn lunatics.

I stared at the ceiling and the darkness and thought about what Lars had said. Not the demon part—Lars did that to everybody—but the bit about the Nairobi Trio.

My God. He's right. That goddamn Lars is right.

It all began to come together.

19. Purgatory

The snow outside the window was disappearing and the world was turning brown again. I had no calendar in my room, so I couldn't cross off the days with a fat red marker. In fact, there were no calendars to be seen anywhere in the ward. Only that single, slow-moving clock, for the other inmates and the nurses to determine when it was time for the next pill or cigarette. I hadn't had the foresight, back in November, to start keeping track of the days with a series of hatch marks on the wall, the way Cagney might've.

In the beginning, I thought I'd be there only for a couple days; the idea of leaving two or three scratches on the wall before I checked out was just stupid. Back then, the days were measured by visits from the dinner cart, and weeks by my Saturday head-butts with Spellman; but those measurements had fallen away, as each one became the same as the last. Dinner and lunch were indistinguishable from breakfast, except for the fact that breakfast came with syrup.

My digital watch, which, along with the approximate

time, would give me the date and a miniature world map
with the designated zones (so I could see, at the touch of
a button or two, what time it was in Istanbul), had long
since died on me. I'd concluded that it had something to
do with the abnormal and extreme electrochemical activity on the surface of my flesh. I never mentioned that to
anybody.

To this day, new watches I wear burn out in a matter
of weeks, and replacement batteries in about the same
amount of time. Even wind-up watches frazzle and gum
up inside. On the ward, I still wore the dead watch every
day, just as I still wore my street clothes and my hat.

Wearing that dead watch and the fedora indoors probably helped a lot to convince the medical staff that I was
well on the road to recovery. People would see the watch
and ask me what time it was, and I'd look at it reflexively,
before admitting, sheepishly, "I really don't know."

The Nairobi Trio wouldn't leave my head. I hummed their
theme song to myself as I sat in my chair or made stabs at
exercise in my strolls around the day room. It kept me
going. Not only did it have an uncomplicated, bouncy
rhythm; it represented a simple, profound truth that no
one else was privy to. It was my own tiny secret, one nobody else would understand, even if I tried to explain it to
them.

Of course, I imagine my humming the same tune over and over as I paced the room wasn't helping me convince anyone of my unshakable sanity, either.

I'd walk from Gus and Edna's corner, past Jack and Mary and Eddie and Chaim in the day room, to the empty couch by the unguarded doors, all the while humming, "*Mi, so, la—re, fa, me, so—do, me, do, fa, re—so! so! . . .*" then turn around and head back to Gus and Edna.

Nobody was sure whether Gus and Edna were sleeping together at night; they'd become quite an item over the past few weeks, though I had never seen them actually touch each other, or even look at each other. People liked to think they were sleeping together, though: the insane are a pretty dirty-minded bunch. During the day Gus had his riding to attend to, so any naughty business was out of the question then. Still, people liked to talk, spreading fabulous tales of the things they'd seen the two of them doing.

Apart from the speculation, sex wasn't much of a concern where I was. The male-to-female ratio was about four to one, and while none of the women was a beauty queen, the men weren't exactly prizes, either. Nor did I see much evidence of homosexual activity. Darin and Peter might've been gay, but I had no real evidence of that. They certainly dressed well enough to make a man suspicious. With the possible exception of the two couples, the patients seemed content with masturbation, and even that they mostly kept to themselves. Only occasionally would someone—Chaim—forget and drop his pants in the day room.

This place wasn't like a college dorm—you didn't hang out in other patients' rooms. I never once saw anybody invite another patient to his or her room for whatever reason, carnal or otherwise. If people were in the mood to talk or play a game, they went to the day room. If a patient stayed in his own room, it meant he was in no mood to be disturbed. I never saw the inside of another patient's room. I never found out whether other people's rooms had walls and windows like mine.

Certain patients I saw only briefly, when the meal carts showed up, so I knew that quite a few people—people I knew nothing about—never left their rooms, except to grab a tray. What sorts of carnality they might've been up to, I cannot say. Nobody seemed to care much.

Myself, I kept frustration at bay by walking and humming.

I figured I had no choice but to explain Lars's revelations in rational, logical, clear terms to Spellman when the time came—which would be Saturday morning, ten-thirty sharp, as always.

The morning of the meeting, I sat in my chair by the window, knee bouncing, anxious. I was beginning to wish that I did smoke cigarettes. It would help the time pass. Just as well, though—the room was heavy with blue-gray clouds of smoke all day long as it was. I only had to sit back, inhale deeply, and pretend.

I rehearsed my explanation in my head, edited it down to three minutes, so there would be time for a question-and-answer period when I was finished:

I had taken that overdose—I choked down all those pills and all that burning scotch—in response to a life of circular repetition. Eating breakfast, putting on socks, taking a shower, sweeping the floor, locking and unlocking doors, day after day. Without some drastic action, there was no escaping. My monotonous life would continue, and it would never end. At least that's what I told myself.

The Nairobi Trio was trapped in a microcosm of the same world. The same simple, mechanical motions to the same simplistic tune, over and over. Repeatedly, the conductor ape got pounded on the head with those drumsticks. He would be frustrated by it—as you could see from his actions and his eyes—but he could never avoid it or put a stop to it. Those drumsticks always got him on the head, even after he thought he had them beat.

At the end of every sketch, his only recourse, his only escape from the frustration, was to move, to stand up and break the cycle. He'd take a few steps and smash a vase over the drummer's head, or collar the other two apes and crack their skulls together. That's how each sketch ended—with a singular, if ineffectual, act of violence. The next week, they'd be back, miming the same song, the drummer pounding again on the conductor's head.

I had escaped one world of mundane repetition by trying to kill myself—a failed, ineffectual act of violence—only to land myself in another world of mundane and unending repetition in the psych ward. I had been trying to escape the boredom, but had only found more of it on the other side, and in much more profound doses. All I had done, in the end, was to jump from one Nairobi Trio sketch into another, from one week to the next. Trying to quit the game had done me no good whatsoever. So what the hell was I supposed to do now?

Instead of waiting for the question-and-answer session, maybe I'd whack Spellman over the head with a vase after I explained everything.

At ten twenty-six, by the clock above the nurses' station, Jason came around the corner and gestured at me. I stood up and followed him down the hall.

He hadn't talked to me much since the night of the tour, and when he did, it was in abrupt, necessary-information-only terms, strictly orderly to patient. That was fine. I'm still not sure what he was expecting out of me, or why he gave me the tour in the first place, unless what he'd said that night was true—that he just wanted someone to know what was going on. Perhaps he expected me to be out a lot sooner than this, too. That's what I preferred to believe, though I could imagine a hundred alternative, more sinister reasons: he might have been trying to scare some broken glass out of me, or preparing me for an inevitable blast of hot electricity through the brain.

Whatever his reason for taking me on the tour, and whatever his reason for ignoring me since, and treating me like any other loon, I'd deal with it. He didn't want to talk, so we wouldn't talk. Instead, once a week he'd gesture to me from the nurses' station, and in silence I'd follow a few steps behind him down the hallway to meet with Spellman.

This morning, when we reached the door, he knocked lightly twice as always, turned the knob, peeked in, then pushed the door open further.

When I walked in, Spellman was sitting at the desk.

"Hello, Mr. Knipfel."

"Hello, Dr. Spellman."

Jason took his seat by the door, and I took mine at the round table. Spellman stood up, walked around the desk, and sat opposite me. We shook hands across the tabletop as we always did—a useless bit of formality.

"How are you today?" Spellman asked, more friendly, it seemed, than usual.

"Doing just fine," I told him. "Had an interesting encounter with Lars the other night—" Since we only had ten minutes, I might as well get into things as quickly as possible.

"Well"—he cut me off, and picked up my file—"before you tell me about Lars, I have some news for you."

My stomach twisted a few millimeters to the right, the way it had at our first meeting.

A shrink announcing that he has "news" is like an oncologist telling you over the phone that he has "concerns," or cops knocking on your door because there's a "problem." Either Jason was about to muscle me across the hall for some electroshock or they were going to put me on Thorazine and turn me into a vegetable like so many of my fellow inmates, or they were going to give me a roommate. Any one of those options would be reason to talk to Jack about obtaining a piece of glass and getting myself the hell out of there for good.

"Yeah?"

"We're going to move you."

Shit. Not "release you," not "send you home," not even send me across the hall or give me a roommate. Just "move" me. I had no idea what he meant, but I didn't like the sound of it.

"But I enjoy where I am—" I started. "I mean, the walls are crazy, but—"

"You don't understand," he cut me off again. "We want to move you upstairs, to the open ward."

"Oh."

"We're not allowed to keep you here much longer, unless you seem dangerous, or are in a situation like Gus out there—and have no sustained contact with reality."

Funny, I'm beginning to think Gus has a better grasp on reality than any of us do. He's the only one on the ward with a girlfriend.

"It's a state regulation."

"So when's this supposed to happen?"

"As soon as possible. This afternoon. They're getting things ready for you up there right now."

"Well." I sat back in my chair. "This is all very sudden. You caught me off guard."

"I thought it was about time. I can see you've made tremendous progress."

I couldn't tell whether he was trying to be ironic, whether he was serious, or if he was talking straight out his ass. The entire time I'd been there, every week had been the same: "I'm not convinced," or "You seem to be doing *too* well, if you understand me." Never a peep about "progress" of any kind. Even a week before, it was, "Your sanity is all an act." Now, with the state nipping at his heels, I'd made "tremendous progress." And just in the past few days, too.

"Thank you, Dr. Spellman." I wondered if he could tell that I was most definitely being ironic.

"You should start getting your things together. A nurse will come for you when they're ready."

"I'll do that. Any idea how long they'll want to keep me up there?"

"That's for them to decide."

Great.

I stood and shook Spellman's hand again, wishing quietly that I had the means at my disposal to hurt him in some way. Not physically, necessarily—yet in some profound way, I wanted to steal from him what he had stolen from me these past months.

Determining what that was, exactly, what it was I might've lost, would be the next order of business.

After Jason opened the door for me, I shook his hand, too.

"Thanks for your help," I said.

"Sure," he replied.

When I stepped into the hallway, a bleak desolation slid over me. I could feel my guts sinking and something dark crowding in my head. I walked to my room slowly, trying to take in all the details. The fire extinguisher inside the locked glass cabinet. The small brown diamond patterns on the tiled floor. The dirty-pink walls. The fluorescent lights overhead.

It was coming to an end. Though I kept telling myself, when I could, that I was having a good time, I'm not sure I ever fully believed it until now. I was going to miss the ward.

Despite my complaints, now that I was leaving, I was frightened about what I might eventually face outside. That day I'd gotten the pass, things had been fine, for the most part. Hearing noises, smelling smells had been invigorating—but I hadn't been in my apartment for fifteen minutes before I could feel something going wrong. I'd gotten used to this place, and it had been months since I'd had to make a meal for myself or take the bus. I hadn't touched money in all this time, and wondered whether I still knew how to count change.

But first I had the open ward to contend with. The rest of the world would come after I got out of there. Maybe the open ward would give me an opportunity to test my Nairobi Trio theory.

I'd been in open wards before; after the business with the wrists, I was put in one. While the name sounded less threatening, open wards could sometimes be rougher than locked wards, given the chance.

I wouldn't be up there too long, if I didn't do or say something that got me booted back down here. I reminded myself to keep my damn mouth shut. If I could do that much, I'd be fine.

It took me only a few minutes to pack. A few clothes, my book, toothbrush and deodorant and shampoo. When I appeared at the nurses' station, wearing my coat and carrying an overnight bag, asking kindly for my electric razor and shoelaces and whatever else of mine was being held, and explained that I was "going away now," the nurse almost skipped to the back to retrieve the shoe box full of contraband.

I put on my belt, laced my shoes, and shoved the razor into my bag, then decided to make a final round of the day room to say my good-byes. I felt like I was in the final color scene of *The Wizard of Oz*, and my throat tightened. Most of these people had no idea where they were or what a pencil sharpener was, let alone who I was. I knew them, though, and some had come to mean a great deal to me these past months.

In a strange and funny way, a few of these lunatics had kept me sane, and I would miss them.

I started in Gus's corner, where he was still pedaling away, trying to escape. Maybe he had already.

"Gus," I said, as he rocked back and forth, legs never stopping, sweat slicking his hair to his forehead. "Gus, you're gonna kill yourself on this thing." I didn't even know whether that was his real name.

Not a word from him—not that I expected any. A few minor grunts, but they had nothing to do with me.

When I reached out and touched his shoulder lightly, his head snapped around, his eyes dark and wild and empty. I jerked my hand away, afraid he might snap at me, and his head swiveled back into position. Down on the floor, Edna was sitting and rocking slightly. She never quite got into it the way Gus did. Maybe in her mind, it was Revlon executives rather than demons who were pursuing her, either to punish her for misusing their products all these years or to offer her free samples.

"Good-bye, Edna." I *knew* that wasn't her real name,

but it didn't matter. I called her that, and a few other patients had picked it up. I squatted and looked into her rov-
ing eyes. There was nothing there. She never knew that I
was in the room from day one, and wouldn't know or care
that I had left.

This was all pointless.

I was trying to say good-bye to crazy people in a heartfelt way, as if they were old school chums, as if we had
been living in the same world and had survived the same
experiences. As if we all spoke the same fucking language.
What kind of craziness was I trying to make work, here?
Whatever my attempts to believe otherwise, you don't get
to "know" the insane—not at all, not in the way others are
used to. You can get to know their behavioral patterns,
and recognize them that way, but you never really know
who's behind those eyes. Especially the people on meds, as
most of these people were. There wasn't anyone behind
those eyes to know.

I felt a certain amount of guilt as I said good-bye.
There were people who had checked into and out of the
ward on a slow but regular basis, and most did so in silence. We hardly noticed them while they were there, and
they never said a word when they left. Some people who
were there, understandably, didn't want to admit they
were, to themselves or anyone else. I was afraid it might
look as if I were gloating, showing off the fact that I was
getting out, even if it was only to go to another ward.

I didn't want anybody to think I considered myself

better than they were. I was going to miss them, and I wanted them to know that. That's all I was after.

I had the impression that any family or friends my neighbors might have had couldn't give a rat's ass about them. They never visited, and obviously didn't want to care for them at home. I didn't blame anyone for that—who would want these people around the house day after day?

I had spent a lot of my time on the ward struggling with the very notions of sanity and insanity—specifically, and curiously, which I would choose for myself. Often I was convinced that I belonged on the ward. I belonged six levels underground, much more than I belonged on the streets again. At other times I knew I had to be let out, so I'd be free to go to bars and bookstores and movie theaters, should I choose to. Yet even if I did decide that I belonged on the ward, that I wanted to be around these folks for a good long time, it was never clear that they wanted me around. At least according to Jack, and he was the closest thing I had to an honest friend there.

I didn't belong much of anywhere, it seemed, but that was okay. I could accept that. Even prefer it that way. Still, I felt a certain bond with a few of the patients, even if they didn't, even if we couldn't really communicate with one another. We had ridden out the winter in the ward together, and that was enough for me.

I skipped Eddie, that greasy paranoid bastard—I wouldn't miss him, and I'm sure he would be glad to have one less person whose motives to suspect—and poked my head into the TV room. I figured I would find Lars there. I hadn't talked to him since that Ernie Kovacs evening, and I wanted to thank him; it didn't matter that he'd probably accuse me of being one of Satan's low-level minions.

"Anyone seen Lars?" I asked the room as a whole.

"*Shhhhh!*" a half-dozen voices shot back at me.

I looked around and didn't see him. Saturday-morning cartoons were well under way, so I backed out quietly and closed the door.

Jack was sitting at his table, smoking what the ashtray indicated was his eighth cigarette of the morning. I stuck my hand out, but he ignored it. Maybe he just didn't see it.

"Hey, Jack, you know what happened to Lars?"

"Lars." It was sort of a question.

"Yeah, big blond guy? Religious? Has a beard."

An interminable pause, as expected, before Jack said, "Away."

"Away? When the hell did that happen?"

Jack was struggling with the words. This was a side effect of his medication. His lips and tongue kept moving, but nothing came out. Finally he managed, "Yesterday."

"Well, where'd he go? How did I miss it?"

Jack shrugged and kept smoking. Stupid questions on my part.

"Well, Jack. I guess I'm going away, too. Moving me upstairs."

He made a small noise in his throat. I flopped my bag on the table and sat down next to him, inhaling the smoke, sweating in my coat and hat. We didn't say anything more.

And as everybody's morning meds kicked in, a silence fell over the room.

I waited an hour until a nurse showed up to take me away. Before we went upstairs, I had to sign several forms at the nurses' station. I didn't bother to read them, and still have no idea what they were about. I thought briefly about the trouble I might be getting myself into—who knew what the forms might claim I'd agreed to—but I ignored the possibilities and signed. Oh, well. Once I'd finished, I walked to the front doors with the transit nurse. I stopped and took a last look around.

It was exactly as it had appeared on the day I arrived. Same dirty-pink paint on the walls, same clouds of smoke, same tables, same ashtrays, same couch (empty now), mostly the same people. It had been home for a while, and it had been a good one. I was sad to see it go. Only now, having reached the point where I could look back on it as a completed memory, did I understand how good it had been.

There was a wheelchair waiting for me in the hallway.

The open ward was the arena where, in theory, patients were allowed to check themselves in and out as they pleased, roam about like free-range chickens, without all those burdensome court orders and directives from families and doctors. It was a few levels above the locked ward—still hidden, but more part of the hospital proper, it seemed.

One of the first things that struck me as I was wheeled off the elevator was the lack of windows. At least none that was immediately apparent. And getting out wasn't nearly as easy as I had been led to believe. You still needed a key to escape, but up here, the key was for the elevator instead of the doors.

While my previous home reminded me of a grade-school cafeteria or a small-town coffee shop, the open ward was more like the front office of a failing midsized insurance company. There was olive-green carpeting on the floor, and beige walls. Instead of being sensibly located and nearly soundproofed, appointed with comfy chairs and a big plexiglass window—easily avoidable if you wanted to avoid it—the television room here *was* the day room.

There was no escaping the incessant noise, the car commercials, the laugh tracks, the insipid commentators. There'd be no reading here, just some skimming through coverless outdated women's magazines. Even in the private rooms down the hall, you couldn't get away from the drone of the television. After having watched almost no TV for so long, finding myself bombarded with it was too horrible to comprehend. I had left a quiet world for one of eternal screeching. The noise drilled into my head, and I wouldn't be able to remedy the ache until I got out, because I still couldn't bring myself to swallow pills. While my fellow patients happily gulped their Thorazine and their Stelazine by the handful, I couldn't force down a couple lousy Tylenol; the very thought of it drove the bile up into my throat.

I had to sign more forms—which I also didn't read—at the smaller and less active front desk of the open ward. Another middle-aged social worker, who never gave me her name, led me down the carpeted hallway to my new room. No patients sat in the hallways, none wandered aimlessly about. I'd noticed a few sitting in front of the television, but that was it.

When we reached my room, the social worker made me clean out my pockets, but didn't take my belt or shoelaces from me. Apparently satisfied that I wasn't going to hurt myself, she left, and I looked around.

Instead of something out of Lovecraft or Escher, my new room was a simple, windowless white-walled box, with more of the olive carpeting on the floor. I felt like a claims adjuster on his inaugural day of work; I'd just been shown to my cubicle, and my first order of business was to decide where to keep my pencil cup and hang my joke-a-day calendar.

This wasn't looking good at all.

Another major difference here was the bed. In the locked ward, with the exception of the Time-Out Room, we had regular twin beds. Here, in the relaxed, friendlier open ward, we were given hospital beds three feet off the ground, with bars on the sides. Were they there to prevent us from rolling out of bed at night and falling to our deaths? Or were they there to make things simpler if the doctor needed to strap us down?

I figured this was the type of place people checked into when the stress of working at a major investment firm got to them, or when they wanted to take a break from their cocaine habit (or both). For those folks' peace of mind, bars on the beds made the place look more like a real hospital than a cheap hotel.

Worse news still was that I didn't have a private bath-

room. The communal bathrooms were down the hall. I
didn't peek in the women's, but I did determine that the
men's had a tub and a shower, three urinals, and two stalls,
neither of which had a door. There were communal showers in the Madison psych ward I had been a few years earlier; I never used them. I washed my hair and upper body
in the sink, and left it at that. Fortunately, I wasn't there
long enough for my stench to become too noticeable. At
my college dorm in Chicago, I got up at four every morning so I wouldn't have to share the shower with anyone.
It's just a thing of mine. All through school in Green Bay,
I never once showered after gym class. It was better to
spend the rest of the day smelling a little humid and rank
than put myself through ritualistic nude humiliation.

Well, if it worked in junior high, it would work here.
I wasn't about to find out firsthand what cruel forms towel
snapping and other tortures would take in the hands of
the insane. Until I learned how long I'd be staying, I felt
comfortable knowing that I'd showered that morning.

Apart from the whine of the television, the hall outside my room was quiet. I wasn't sure how to lower the
bars on the sides of my bed, wasn't sure even how to get
into it, period, without some sort of footstool. I'd work
that out later.

There were no chairs in my new room, either. Everything about the open ward, it seemed, was maddening.
After unpacking a few things, I had no choice but to ven-

ture back into the land of the television to sit down, ask for help, do anything at all.

I returned to the desk in the reception area. "Hi," I said to the nurse. "Um, I just got here, and I was wondering how I might go about making a phone call."

"Who are you going to call?" she asked, without looking up from her paperwork.

"I thought I'd call my folks, let them know that I'd been moved. I've been downstairs for quite a while—I doubt anyone told them I was being moved up here. I just found out I was moving this morning."

She shoved the phone toward me, an old-fashioned black rotary job.

I picked up the receiver. "Thanks. Do I need to do anything special to get out?"

"Be good and act normal." She smirked at her joke.

"Yes, well, we'll see if that does the trick up here." I dialed the phone and heard my dad on the other end.

"Hey. They've moved me upstairs," I told him. "Into the open ward."

"That's *great*. Does that mean you'll be out soon?"

"I'm not sure. I'll ask. Hold on." I cupped my hand over the speaker. "Excuse me?" I said to the nurse again. "Does being moved up here mean that I'm going to be getting out soon, do you think?"

"That's up to the doctor to decide."

"I guess I figured that." I took my hand away to talk

to my dad again. "Okay, it's unclear. Nurse here says it's up to the doctor, and I'm not sure when he's going to be here."

"Well, you let us know, okay?"

"You know I will. I love you—and be sure and tell Mom I love her, too." I hung up, and moved the phone back to the nurse. "Thanks, again."

I looked around the room. The chairs and couches were arranged for easy viewing of the television, which was poised in the middle of the room, volume turned up high. I wondered whether they let patients watch wrestling up here. That seemed unlikely without any obvious barriers between the patients and nurses. But who knew? Maybe the nurses up here packed heat.

I turned back to the woman at the desk. "Sorry to bother you again, but I was wondering—what do I do now? I mean, when do I see the doctor?"

"Whenever he's here."

I sighed and rolled my eyes. "Okay, let's try it this way: Any idea when the doctor might be here?" I tried to keep my voice calm.

Remember, keep your yap shut.

"Probably not until Monday, unless there's an emergency."

That's right, it was Saturday. I looked at my watch, then around the room for a clock, but didn't see any. I couldn't even try to estimate the hour by the light outside, since there were no windows.

"Do you know what time it is?"

Now she sighed, and looked at her own watch. "Three o'clock." She went back to her work.

"Ma'am, I'm sorry to keep bothering you, I know you're busy and all, but is there anyone here I can talk to? I mean, just to learn procedures and find out how I'm going to get dinner tonight, that sort of thing?"

She slammed her papers down with angry disgust and picked up her own phone, then hit a button.

"Jean?" she spat. "There's a new patient here who wants a *tour* or something." She paused. "Fine. Thanks. I'll tell him." She hung up. "Someone'll be out in a minute. Have a seat."

"Great, thanks," I told her through a grimacing smile.

I went over toward the television. There was nowhere else to go. A few other patients, in matching hospital clothes, stared dully at the screen. Some dreadful movie was on.

I plopped myself near the end of a couch, as far from the nurses' desk as possible, near a man in a wheelchair.

"Hello there," I offered.

He didn't respond—just continued staring at the screen. Or at least toward the screen. I was used to that, and I leaned closer and asked quietly, "So what do I need to know about this place?"

While I had never been very sociable, never much of a talker, I understood—especially in the locked ward—

that if I wanted the skinny on something, I had to talk to people. That's why I'd started talking to Jack; if Jack knew the answer, he'd let me in on it. While most people, I'd come to believe, were inveterate liars (especially the insane), if I asked enough of them, I could generally piece the truth together well enough.

This man, though, wasn't being very cooperative. He stared at the screen, not acknowledging my presence.

Another victory for drug therapy. Keeps the information in all the proper hands.

It took me a second to see that his wrists were strapped to the arms of his wheelchair. He couldn't move the damn thing by himself even if he wanted to. I looked at the other faces in the room: there wasn't one that, on the surface at least, appeared capable of speech at the moment.

I was in a land of the dead. The folks downstairs might've been crazy, but a few of them had at least a bit of life left in them, some flash and sparkle and spunk, even if it made no sense.

Am I romanticizing already?

I gave up on trying to pry any information out of this crowd and settled in to wait for this Jean person.

Half an hour later, to judge from the commercial breaks on the television, the social worker who had checked me in reappeared.

"My name's Jean," she said, as if we had never met before. "What is it that you're wondering?" There was nothing kindly about her. Not even an attempt at feigned kindliness. She just wanted to answer my questions as quickly as possible and get the hell away from me. Maybe she'd been given reason to fear transfers from the locked ward.

"Well, where do I begin? How long am I going to be here?"

"That's for the doctor to decide."

"Yeah, I know. My question is, is this usually just a necessary stepping-stone on the way out, or am I going to be here awhile?"

"That's for the doc—"

"Yeah, okay, fine," I interrupted. "And I don't see him until Monday, right?"

"Probably."

"So what do I do until then?"

"Relax."

I sighed. "Ma'am, I don't want to appear rude or belligerent or anything like that, not at all, but I've been relaxing for some time now, downstairs. Long time, to be honest . . . Okay, let me put it this way: I know where this room is, I know where my room is, I know where the bathroom is—is there anyplace else I should know about?"

"Not that I can think of."

"Okay, well, where do we eat?"

Calmly and carefully—she, like Ms. Cartwright, was speaking as if she was dealing with some mildly retarded child who just wasn't getting it—she said, "Most patients on this floor choose to eat in their rooms."

"Uh-huh. Well, then, could you maybe explain how I'd do that with no chair or table or anything?"

She looked puzzled. "You don't have a chair?"

I shook my head.

"We'll see about getting you one. Now if that's it, I should get back to work. It's just been a crazy day around here."

I cocked an eyebrow.

"One more thing about meals," I started, before she could run off again, "do the folks in the kitchen know I've moved?"

"We'll find out for you," she said as she walked away.

"Hey!" I shouted after her. "What about smoking?"

"No smoking," she replied over her shoulder. "This is a smoke-free environment."

I returned to the couch for a while, and sat next to the vegetable in the wheelchair. Eventually my attention turned back to the television. A commercial for the local news came on, and a newsreader breathlessly promised that at six he would be delivering complete coverage of "one of the worst plane crashes in modern aviation history."

There had been a news blackout in the locked ward, intentional or not, I didn't know. No newspapers, no magazines, and so no incessant flood of reports on the awful things that happened to people on the outside every day. I never saw the patients in the television room watch the evening news. Before coming to the hospital, I'd been obsessed with the news—murders, earthquakes, wars, plane crashes—but once I made my decision, all that faded.

Only now did I vaguely recall that a war had been getting under way that morning so long ago. I didn't remember who was involved. I'd hear about it eventually. Downstairs I hadn't missed the news, hadn't cared about it in the least, but here, already I could feel the old craving for savagery and trauma returning.

This news of a plane crash seemed promising. A nice welcome back into the world. I would try to catch the report later, if I could figure out what time it was.

I looked again at the people sitting with me. Television news or not, I was feeling more isolated from the world than I ever had downstairs. Better to explore my new surroundings further. I strolled to the elevators. Hell, I was dressed, I wouldn't be leaving that much behind. Certainly nothing I couldn't replace. Why not just walk away? Amble out of the hospital as if I'd been there visiting a sick relative.

I could call my folks from a pay phone outside, have them come pick me up, then speed off into the twilight. I didn't have a quarter on me for the phone, but I could bum one. You always hear about people walking away from prison work farms or mental institutions, so evidently it could be done. I mean, this wasn't a hospital for the criminally insane or anything—people checked themselves in and out all the time. It would be no big deal.

I'd never considered running away when I was downstairs. I didn't care about what was happening in the world, and never thought of escape, except in terms of other people, like Edna. There was no point to it. I was where I belonged. I didn't always like it, and I dreamed of what might be awaiting outside, but I knew it was where I belonged. I had always perceived myself as an outsider, and being down there proved that I was right. I couldn't get much more outsider than being locked away in the Bin. Unless I had landed myself in prison or joined the freak show, and even those seemed more like real communities than the madhouse. Besides, on the locked ward, I probably wouldn't know how to get outside once I got beyond the locked doors.

I turned away from the elevators and put the idea out of my head. I'd need a key to go anywhere, anyway.

Shit. Open ward, my ass.

I'd concentrate on the more immediate problem, of getting into my new bed.

It hadn't taken long to realize things here were worse than they had been mere hours earlier. I was stupid enough to believe I was being given a gracious hand up, getting boosted a step closer to the outside. Instead, everything was colder, more alienating and degrading. Of course, maybe in that way it was a step closer to the outside—except that on the outside I didn't have to worry about communal showers. And I had a place to sit. And I was able to get into my own bed, no matter how drunk I was. You couldn't even *smoke* here. I wasn't a smoker myself, but that didn't matter. What's the point of being crazy if you can't smoke? I didn't have a window to look out of, no promise of something better. No promise of anything outside these sterile white walls.

My plastic dinner tray was delivered on the cart with all the others, but when it arrived I still had no chair and had spoken to no one else. I ate standing up at the narrow counter in my room. I filled out the breakfast menu slip and returned the empty tray to the cart. Then I sat down in front of the television to catch the news about the airplane crash. The footage showed billowing clouds of black smoke pouring from a shattered hull.

When it came time to go to sleep, I circled the bed looking for an opening. There were no bars across the foot of the bed, so that's where I started.

I bent at the waist, grabbed two handfuls of blanket, and tried to pull myself the rest of the way up, but succeeded only in yanking most of the bedding off. I gathered it and tossed it back on the bed, bent again, and tried to hoist myself using the bars on either side. After all these months, my arms were just too weak.

Christ Almighty, if someone opened that door right now, I'd be trussed up and shipped back downstairs faster than I can spit.

I felt like a midget, or a child. I took a step back and tried to jump in, but this time succeeded only in stubbing a toe and whacking my right shoulder on the cold metal of the safety bar. I bit my tongue to keep from yelping, and limped about the bed, rubbing my shoulder. I could find no obvious solution.

These fuckers. Probably got a closed-circuit camera set up in here. Probably laughing at me.

Finally, what must've been forty-five minutes later, I tested the bars to make sure they'd hold my weight, and lifted my left leg. I secured a reasonable foothold and bounced on my right leg, the way I'd seen Mary try to climb the counter downstairs. Luckily I was slighter than she was, and on the fifth or sixth try I was able to slump myself clumsily over the top bar.

I lay on my back on the cold mattress and that pile of bedding, looking at the ceiling and breathing hard. My technique may not have won me any awards, but I'd done it—I'd beaten the bed. At least for one night, I'd beaten something. Then I realized that I hadn't shut off the lights. I almost wept.

For the rest of that night, and most of the next day—which I spent in my room, sitting on the floor—I couldn't shake the memories of those first three days after the overdose.

I hadn't been able to escape those memories since I'd entered the hospital. After the intensive care unit, I could try to hide them away, pretend they didn't happen. I usually had other things to occupy me. When I didn't, though, there the memories were again. They seemed so real. Most dreams fade after a few minutes or hours—they wait until they can creep out in the darkness again. But memories like these are different. My body had been in the hospital all that time—I was pretty sure of that, at least— but something else, some other part of me that I hesitate to call a "soul," had gone to Hell. Even after I came back around, well, things didn't seem all that different.

Of course, thinking that it was a real place I had been, a collection of real things I had done, might well be taken as evidence of the "psychotic break" the doctors had talked about. I knew it would be unwise to discuss anything of the sort with the new doctor when I met with him on Monday. I hadn't told Spellman, and I wouldn't tell this new guy. There would be nothing about it in my file. They wouldn't be able to use it against me.

No, this I would keep to myself. Besides, I'd been able to sense what was happening to my body at almost every moment. Virtually everything that happened had a basis in what the shrinks, to make things simple for themselves, wanted to call "reality." Trips in police cars and ambulances, that charcoal drink, my attempts to rip out the catheter.

Still, with all that, as much as I could work out a literal, earthly timeline for myself, a lot remained unanswered. What about my Grandpa Carrol in his Indian wig giving me the thumbs-up sign on the bus? Was he telling me that I was going to be okay, or was he letting me know I had crossed over into his world? What about the Nazis, and all that opera?

I'd never be able to bring up these sorts of questions with any shrink. I wouldn't even be able to bring them up with a theologian, should I ever have the inkling. It would sound like crazy talk. Like pointing out the impossible angles in my room downstairs.

By Sunday evening, I had convinced myself that it had, indeed, been nothing more than a fetid stew of noxious chemicals swirling around my brain, that I had taken the hazy reality I was able to perceive and run amok with it. Those parts of my trip I couldn't explain away logically I chose to ignore.

While I could tell myself no, I hadn't really been to Hell, my new circumstances led me to believe that I might possibly be well on my way there now.

On Monday morning, as I was returning my breakfast tray to the cart, the nurse behind the desk told me that Dr. Haverford would like to see me.

"Oh. Good. Um, where do I find him?"

"End of the hall here, last door on your right." She actually smiled what seemed to be an authentically friendly smile. I smiled back and thanked her. Then she picked up the phone to let the doctor know I was on my way.

As with that cretin Spellman, it was the last door on the right. *Last Door on the Right.* Just keep telling yourself: It's only a movie.

I knocked, and a muffled voice ushered me in.

Haverford's office was not nearly as lavish as the communal room where I'd met with Spellman. No big table in the middle, no plush couches. Just a desk and chairs, and curling watercolor prints tacked on the walls. Still no windows. This entire level of the hospital must have been positioned strangely. Maybe that landscape architect wasn't such a genius after all. He could grant a lovely view to someone six levels underground—but the folks up here were left buried.

Haverford was in the middle of eating his own breakfast, off the same kind of tray the patients used. That he had his food delivered with the rest of ours I took as a good sign. It showed a lack of pretense and a lack of fear on his part. He motioned for me to sit and moved his tray aside.

He wasn't so much hefty as bulky, with glasses and a graying beard. The shirt under his lab coat was open at the neck.

"I'd offer to shake hands," he said, "but I'm all greasy here."

"That's okay—I'm sorry to've disturbed you."

"Don't worry about it. I wanted to get this over with as soon as possible."

That didn't sound good. He wanted to get the introductions out of the way now. Then he could finish his breakfast in peace. He'd have plenty of time to deal with the nuts and bolts over the ensuing months and years I'd be spending here.

"I went over your file this past weekend." He slid it out from beneath his tray.

"Uh-huh?"

"You were quite the troublemaker."

"Pardon?"

He grinned broadly. "Just kidding."

"Please don't kid with a crazy man. You never know what we'll do."

He paged through the file, then leaned back in his chair and looked at me. "Do you think you're crazy?"

"To be honest, I haven't for quite some time—but I also know that by saying that, I might be getting myself into trouble."

"Yes, I can understand how you might feel that way, given where you were. . . . But to be honest here, Mr., um . . ."

"Knipfel."

"I don't see any evidence of aberrant behavior that would appear to signal that you're a danger to yourself or others. At least not at the present time."

"That's what I've been trying to tell Dr. Spellman for six months."

"Yes, well, Dr. Spellman is a very good doctor."

I was going to offer him long odds on that, but held my tongue.

"So," Haverford went on, "I just don't see any reason to keep you in the hospital any longer."

After I left his office, I went to the front desk and asked if I might make another phone call.

My parents whooped on the other end of the phone when I told them simply, "I'm outta here." Back in my room, I packed up the few things I had bothered to unpack. I put my trench coat on and went out to wait by the television. This time I didn't have anyone to say goodbye to.

I'm finally going home.

My head filled with a mix of glee, anxiety, fear, and happy disbelief.

Was I cured? If so, cured of what? They didn't *do* anything to me down there, or up here. They only kept me comfortably locked away for a while, preparing me for the next time I'd be locked away.

I had lived with the notion, as many angry young men have, that I would end my days in either a prison or a madhouse. And maybe I would, who knew? While I wasn't planning on a trip back here anytime soon, I knew that plans and the lack of plans add up to pretty much the same thing.

Quitting this new Nairobi Trio sketch—whatever it turned out to be over the coming months—wasn't something I had a mind to do just yet. I'd see how it went. If it didn't work out, if it was as ugly as all the others, I'd deal with it in whatever way struck me as appropriate and necessary. With luck, I'd never have to reach that point.

What scared me was that I wasn't sure I had any real choice in the matter. It hadn't felt like a choice in the past, when I took the blade to my flesh or threw back those pills. But I had gotten through the psych-ward sketch and out the other side without blood or cheap violence. So what happens now? Even scarier than the question of my choice in the matter was the fact that the world waiting for me outside was a place I wasn't sure I knew anymore. In a way, I would be walking into it as weakened as when I was buzzed into the locked ward for the first time.

Screw Lacan and Freud and all their hoo-ha about language. That wasn't the point with me. With Gus, maybe, their approaches might've made sense, but not with me. Screw Spellman, too—though I never understood what sort of methodology he thought he was using.

In my case, the solution was much simpler, much more fundamental than the hydraulic churnings around my unconscious. As with everything else, the game was one of survival. And the key to my surviving in this next new world was clear: Recognize the skit I was in before I got too far into it. Figure out who—or what—was holding the drumsticks over my head early enough so I could dodge them, before they caved in the back of my skull. They got me too many times, and I wouldn't have any choice but to smash some glass, whether over someone else's head or my own couldn't be said until the time came. And if that time did come, I was in for it either way.

If, as had been the case in the past, the drumsticks consisted of boredom and repetition, then the answer was to keep moving, and keep the things around me moving, too, otherwise they might stop moving for a good long time. If Lars, and those first three days in the hospital, had taught me anything, it was to keep my legs in motion, and keep my eyes darting back and forth. If I didn't, the Nazis, or the mob, or the drumsticks would be there before I could do anything about them. It might mean a little trouble, but trouble's better than oblivion.

I'd been sitting still far too long.

My folks arrived at the hospital half an hour after I called. We signed the release papers—I still didn't read them—and a nurse rode with us down to the lobby. Or was it up to the lobby? She stayed in the elevator as we got off, and turned the key again to leave. I watched her as the doors closed.

It was nearly springtime. The day was cold and the sky a Minneapolis slate gray. I was thin and white after those months inside with so little movement and nothing but fluorescents shining on me. The wind sheared through me like a rusty machete. I shivered, but it felt good to breathe air that wasn't processed. I enjoyed hearing my footsteps on something other than tile. We walked to the parking lot, I crawled into the backseat of my parents' Ford, and we started toward my apartment. Before we'd gone too far, I asked if we could pull into a gas station.

"Sure," my dad said. "Why?"

"I need to get something." I left it at that. A few blocks later, he pulled into a Shell station.

"I'll be right back." I climbed from the car with the two bucks I had borrowed from him and ran to the station.

When we got to my apartment, I'd sit my parents down and tell them why I'd done what I'd done, and why I didn't think I'd have to do it again. I could do that now.

A minute later, I was walking back to the car, ripping the cellophane off a pack of Pall Mall straights.

I hoped they'd understand.

21. sechs

Several hours had passed, and still Laura hadn't returned. I walked to the crest of the hill and looked over, but there was no sign of either of them. I climbed back down to the boat and set out onto the oval river again.

On the other side of the hill, I saw a cluster of women in colonial garb. I pulled ashore to ask whether they'd seen her.

They hadn't, but pointed toward a cave and said that I might want to look inside. I walked into the cave and found myself in the kitchen of an inn, where bread was baking and several large pots were boiling on top of wood-burning stoves. Nobody in the kitchen knew anything, or if they did, they refused to say so. Frustrated, I lay down on an oak disk about eight feet across, connected to the ceiling by heavy black iron chains. When I looked up, I saw that I had several wires and tubes sticking into my arms, legs, and penis.

I grabbed hold of the wire coming out of my penis.

"Tell me where she is, or I'll tear it out," I threatened

the tough old woman who seemed to be in charge. I had no idea what I was threatening—or whom or why.

She snapped a tight claw onto my wrist and growled at me. "Give it up. She doesn't love you. *Nobody* loves you. Why would she leave you if she loved you?"

I stopped straining, let go of the catheter, and lay down on the wooden disk.

"Oh, take me out of here," I groaned weakly. I wanted nothing more than to die again. It was a pathetic scene.

"You heard him!" the old woman screamed toward the ceiling, "Take him up!"

The chains grew taut, and the disk was slowly, creakily dragged upward, with steam and the smell of baking bread rising above me. I thought I was being lifted into a dining room, but as I approached the ceiling, it pulled open, revealing daylight.

I was strapped down again, but this time to a bed, just inside the roof of a parking ramp. In front of me—in the uncovered area—stood Laura and Tom. She was still dressed like a Valkyrie; he was still dressed like a lumberjack. I was wearing a flimsy hospital gown, and was surrounded by medical personnel and cops.

Laura and Tom both started toward me, yelling something, the words inaudible. Just then, a helicopter appeared above them, descending, blowing their words away.

They kept trying to run toward me, but the helicopter rotor blew them back. I couldn't tell if they were waiting for it or threatened by it.

Everything was too loud, and happening too fast. I couldn't take it anymore—

"STOP IT!"

Silence.

"Just . . . stop it."

I began to make a speech overburdened with Nietzschean and individualistic philosophy. It grew in tempo and rage and force. People stopped what they were doing and listened to me. Nobody had ever listened to me. I kept talking. A few horns in the garage behind me honked in what I guessed to be approval. Cops who'd been standing around doing nothing ran to silence them. Laura and Tom remained where they were, listening.

I kept talking, encouraging people to take responsibility for themselves. I had no idea where the words were coming from. I'd never spoken in this way before.

The cops grabbed hold of the bed and threw me into the back of an ambulance-bus. By now my voice had reached fever pitch. People were applauding. Laura and Tom were applauding. The bus pulled away—and as it did, I knew I'd still failed somehow.

We were driving through Green Bay, and I heard more and more car horns honking. People were waving.

We drove by the prison, and I could see through the

fence and into the yard. Prisoners were dumping straw and leaves out through the bars of their windows. We drove around the city, through downtown, into the suburbs of Allouez and DePere, then back again.

The bus stopped, and my grandfather (who had died the previous year) climbed aboard and sat in one of the front seats. He wore his hair tied in long gray braids, like an Indian in an old western. He looked at me strapped to my bed and gave me a smile and a thumbs-up sign. I returned the gesture as well as I could, my eyes burning with tears. I wanted to talk to him, but he got off at the next stop.

While the parade—or whatever the hell it was— continued, things on the street grew more chaotic and uncontrollable. A garbage can was thrown through a store window, fires were set. What had started as a mild demonstration was turning into a riot. I couldn't have been happier. This was just what I had been hoping for. I wanted the whole fucking planet to burn down.

But then we passed three bodies laid out on the side of the road. They were bicyclists, killed by a driver who had lost control of his car. I knew that ultimately it was my responsibility.

Night came, and bonfires set in the streets and in yards lit our way. My aunt Dorthea got on the bus and gave me a stern look.

"I hope you're happy," she sneered bitterly.

She dragged me out of the bed I was in and strapped

me to a board. I was now immobile. The bus seemed to be driving in circles around the same block, which happened to be the block my parents lived on. Their house, in fact, from what I could tell as we drove past, had been converted into the headquarters for something. I asked for a drink and was given more ice chips. That wasn't enough. I wanted a beer.

I needed to find Laura. I thought she must be in the area someplace. I started asking people on the street as we passed them, shouting my questions out the open window. Nobody had seen her.

Finally, at the top of Allouez Avenue, before the bus turned right onto Webster, I saw an encampment of people by a newsstand, wrapped in blankets and drinking coffee. Tom was there. I yelled to him and he came over. He told me that Laura was okay and had been trying to find me. She was by the newsstand. Before he could go to get her, the bus moved on. I wasn't worried, though—I knew we'd be coming around again in a few minutes.

Suddenly the air was filled with laughter and joy. People were living for the moment, not caring about their jobs the next day, or the troubles they'd had the day before; they were just having fun. Newscasters on the radio were saying that the revolution had spread around the globe. But people in Washington and Moscow, they reported, were determined to put an end to it by whatever means necessary.

The next time we rolled around the block, someone

pulled me out of the bus and left me on the sidewalk. Sometime later, someone else untied me and I could finally stand upright for the first time in several days.

In the distance, a church bell chimed twice. According to a newscaster, this meant that missiles had been launched. People grew quiet. They turned to me, threatening to tear me apart and stomp what was left. This fiasco was entirely my fault.

Before anyone could grab me, the bells chimed again, three times, which meant that the first report had been a false alarm. The mob slipped back into a celebratory mood.

I walked around, talked to people, drank coffee, looked at newspapers—

Then the two chimes tolled again.

Again the threats. The masses, realizing that they were alive, wanted to lynch me.

Then the bells tolled again, five times. Nobody knew what this meant. People seemed more resigned. If the bombs fell, they fell. Fuck it.

But the bombs didn't fall. Still, as the morning light crept over the horizon, the mob didn't seem very happy. They'd had their fun, yes, but now they had to clean up and get their lives back to normal. They were pissed at me for causing such a mess. Newspapers and coffee cups and beer cans littered the streets—and they all had to be picked up.

I gave another speech, telling these people that for

the first time they'd really been alive. They should be thankful. If they weren't—if they were willing to give up everything they had believed in for that one night, just quit and have everything go back to how it was before— then I would leave, and they'd never see me again.

That seemed to be the consensus.

I blacked out again.

When my eyes reopened, I found myself in a hospital once more, but now all the lights were off. Some spotlights from outside crisscrossed through the window in my room and played across the walls and ceiling. Strange blue lights. There was nobody else around—no doctors or nurses or orderlies. The halls were empty. The hospital, I realized, had been evacuated, and in the process, I had been forgotten.

I had to go to the bathroom. I stood up from the bed with wires and tubes still sticking out of my arms and legs and shuffled over to the small porcelain pot behind the blue curtain. As I sat down, sweating and straining, I saw well enough through the window to know why the hospital had been evacuated.

The Aztec god Quetzalcoatl, the winged serpent, had nested on the roof. In the parking lot below, the military and the police were trying to shoot it down while it swooped from its perch and snatched people away.

The next thing I knew, I was rhyming in German.

bibliography

Gollmar, Robert H., *Edward Gein: America's Most Bizarre Murderer*. Delevan, WI: Charles Haliberg, 1981.

Lacan, Jacques, *Écrits: A Selection*, trans. Alan Sheridan. New York: W. W. Norton, 1977.

a c k n o w l e d g m e n t s

I humbly thank the following for their support and assistance:

My remarkable editor at Tarcher, David Groff; my publicist, Ken Siman, who always goes above and beyond; copy editor Anna Jardine, who makes me seem much better than I am; Ken Swezey and Laura Lindgren, who made all things possible; Tony Trachta and Tom Horn for their invaluable technical assistance; my parents, George and Janice Knipfel, as well as Mary, Bob, MacKenzie, and Jordan Adrians; John Strausbaugh, Russ Smith, Maz, Andrey, Bill Monahan, Lisa Kearns, Bax, C. J. Sullivan, Russell Christian, and the rest of the folks at *New York Press;* Peg Tyre and Peter Blauner; Chip Kidd; Dave and Sarah Read, Joe Coleman, Scott Ferguson, Jim Canfield, Mike Walsh, David E. Williams, Suzanne and Peter Ross; the Rios family; Linda, John, Sue, Steve Kersten, Sam, Tom LeGoff, Richard Lane, Waylon Wahl, Reid Paley, Kevin Baier, and the rest of the Hangdogs, Lance Fitzgerald and Lisa Beck, TP, Homer Flynn, and all the fine folks at Cryptic.

I especially thank Morgan Intrieri, whom I love madly. She makes things so very easy.

about the author

Jim Knipfel lives in Brooklyn. He just likes it there, is all.